Joel Stickley is the author of the hit blog "How To Write Badly Well", which has dispensed bad advice to over half a million visitors since its launch. With long-time collaborator Luke Wright, he wrote the book *Who Writes This Crap?* which *The Guardian* called "an inspired piece of parody," and the animated film *Crash Bang Wallow*, which won the NFBC Short Film Award at the 2010 Cannes Film Festival. He is Poet Laureate for the UK county of Lincolnshire and teaches creative writing at the Open University.

D1600163

100 Ways to Write Badly Well

Joel Stickley

Momentum

First published by Momentum in 2012
Pan Macmillan Australia Pty Ltd
1 Market Street, Sydney 2000

A CIP record for this book is available at the National Library of
Australia

100 Ways to Write Badly Well

EPUB format: 9781743340776
Mobi format: 9781743340882
Print on Demand format: 9781743340899

Cover design by Patrick Naoum
Illustrations by Patrick Naoum
Edited by Kylie Mason
Proofread by Hayley Crandell

Macmillan Digital Australia: www.macmillandigital.com.au

To report a typographical error, please email
errors@momentumbooks.com.au

Visit www.momentumbooks.com.au to read more about all our books
and to buy books online. You will also find features, author interviews
and news of any author events.

Table of Contents

Introduction

The phrase 'toilet book' gets bandied around a lot as a derogatory term, but I can think of no human activity better complemented by reading than what happens on toilets. As you allow your body to do its vital work, a book can ensure that your mind is just as stimulated as your lower intestine after the rigours of a hard day. Or, to put it another way: out with one kind of crap, in with another.

In my time as a writer and creative writing tutor, I've noticed something counterintuitive – really bad writing is more fun than really good writing. If I'm given a choice between sitting down with *À la recherche du temps perdu* or a poem that rhymes 'dinosaur' with 'lino floor,' the T. rex in the kitchen is going to win every time. It's in that spirit that I started writing deliberately awful pieces of short fiction. Mixed metaphors, unbelievable plot twists, piles of conflicting adjectives –

anything to escape the tedium of perfectly honed prose. And it was fun – far more fun than agonising over commas for hours at a time. I got carried away. Soon, I found that I'd written hundreds of these things. I had them on a blog. Strangers were sending me their own deliberately bad writing. I was even doing readings of some of the best (by which I of course mean worst) examples. It became obvious that bad writing had an inexplicable momentum of its own and needed to be showcased. Hence this book.

This isn't a how-to guide, although I suppose you could use it as one. Neither is it a serious literary experiment like Raymond Queneau's *Exercises in Style* (although if there are any competition judges or broadsheet reviewers reading, yes it is). Rather, it's a celebration of terrible writing, a chance to luxuriate in the worst excesses of purple prose. It's designed to be dipped into and enjoyed in idle moments. A good example of this might be when you are taking care of important business on the toilet – which I think brings us back to where we started.

Joel Stickley

1

Begin your novel with the protagonist getting out of bed and seeing that it is raining outside, which perfectly mirrors his life.

Jake opened his eyes and heard the rain battering against the outside of the glass window. Well, he thought grimly, it's raining outside, and it's certainly raining in my soul, which is about as inside as you can get!

It had only been seventeen days since he'd lost his job and been dumped by his girlfriend, all of which made him very sympathetic without actually having to establish him as a character. Ever since that fateful day, he had been hearing the *drip drip drip* of his hopes (raindrops) and aspirations (hailstones) tumbling down onto the corrugated iron roof of his memory before disappearing forever down the drain of missed opportunities.

2

Use as many adjectives as you can.

She slowly walked the slow, winding path towards the crooked, run-down old house. With one slow, hesitant hand she bravely, resolutely knocked on the dusty, pock-marked, ancient and frightening door. Slowly, it opened slowly. She slowly poked her brave head through the narrow, foreboding gap.

'Hello?' she slowly queried, bravely.

Just then, suddenly – yet strangely slowly – a terrifying, scary, bone-chilling, face-tingling, stupefyingly mortifying and stultifying, yet oddly inconsequential and subtly fragrant, big, massive, enormous multihued, monochrome monstrosity of epic, legendary, massive, indescribable proportions burst thunderingly from the shadowy, ill-defined, hazy, portentous, generically appropriate yet obviously underdeveloped and self-evidently over-described dark, dark darkness.

'RAAAAAAH!' it roared.

3

Start your novel at least three chapters before the first significant event of the plot.

Alan picks up his slice of toast and bites into it thoughtfully. The crescent shape left by his teeth is like a smaller version of the shark bite Julia will suffer next week, but at the moment, Alan knows nothing about that. The surface of his coffee ripples like a deceptively calm ocean, which, any moment now, sharks will come leaping out of. He slurps it, completely unaware.

So far, there is no sign of his parcel – the new scuba mask with anti-fog coating that will eventually (although not for some days) save his life. There isn't even a postcard from Julia, despite her still, at this point, having enough fingers to write one. He wants to know what the weather is like on the coast before he goes there on Thursday.

Of course, today is Monday, so there's still plenty of time. Maybe a postcard will come tomorrow. Until then, Alan just has to get through his last few days at work, which promise to be mind-numbingly repetitive and predictable, exactly unlike a shark attack.

4

Don't worry about tenses.

I sit at my desk with my head in my hands and sighed. It is only three days until the deadline, I think, and I'm going to have had to finished everything before then. If only I have finish this now, I thought and lean back on my chair. Just then, the phone has rung. I am answering it.

'Hello?' I am going to have asked. It is my editor; he was angry, but not as angry as I remember him being when I am handing in the work late, four days from now.

'Is this work going to have been finished when it is currently the deadline, which, at present, is in the future?' he demanded. 'I am planning to have been waiting for it, as I presently am.'

5

Banish 'said' from your vocabulary.

'I'm afraid she's dead,' unveiled the doctor. A silence settled on the room as the family took this in.

'You're sure?' proclaimed Lois, quietly. The

doctor nodded.

'I'm terribly sorry,' he conversed. 'It was a peaceful end.'

'Did she …' Lois vocalised. 'Did she have any last words?'

'Yes,' nodded the doctor, nodding. 'She epitaphed a few words before she left us. "Tell my children I love them," she stated. Then she recapitulated "all of them", and shortly after that, she went.'

'I can't believe it,' philosophised Lois. 'I can't believe she's gone.'

'I'm so terribly sorry,' the doctor gushed.

'Can I ask a question?' questioned Lois.

'Of course,' dialogued the doctor.

'If we had brought her in sooner,' she began, 'is there anything we could have done,' she continued, 'to give her more time?' she concluded, questioningly.

'I … I'm afraid not,' the doctor ejaculated.

6

Write with half an eye on the market.

The Darknight Academy for witches, wizards, troubled vampires and tragically abused children was just waking up when the screaming started. Secret Agent Sam Glowingly sprang athletically from his bed and reached for his pistol. He had been undercover for three weeks now and this was the first sign of trouble, unless you counted the theft of the Holy Grail the previous week, which he didn't.

Whatever the problem, he was sure he could handle it. He had faced seemingly impossible odds before, like that time his wife had been forced to choose which of their twin daughters to donate a kidney to.

He kicked open the door and found a young orphan vampire-wizard wailing in the corridor outside.

'What's wrong?' he quizzed.

'I've been shockingly yet predictably abused,' sobbed the boy.

7

Misuse apostrophe's.

The last of the suns ray's are fading as the boy's walk with slow and heavy step's toward's their homes'.

'The day's are getting longer,' say's Ross.

'Thats because summers here,' say's Rosss

brother. He sigh's and kicks' a pebble along the paths edge. It rattle's down a drain and disappear's from Rosss view. He raise's hi's eye's to the cloud's and squint's.

'Whatre you'r plan's now schools over?' he say's. His' brother shrug's hi's shoulder's.

'I dont know,' he say's. 'S'ome'thing 's'uper s'pe'c'ia'l.'

8

Create unlikely love interests.

Arianna Milieux, the most widely respected female theologian of her era, watched a leaf fall slowly from one of the tall trees on the boulevard outside. The way it fell – drifting first one way, then the other – put her in mind of what she had been reading the previous day regarding the Miltonic concept of predestination.

She was just reaching for a pen when something bright caught her eye. Between the trees, she could see the garish colours of a circus convoy, complete with elephants, acrobats and jugglers. What really took her breath away, though, was the sight of the man who walked behind this acrobatic spectacle, calmly pacing along the boulevard as if he owned the city and everything in it. Even from a distance, she could see the piercing blue of his eyes, the firm set of his jaw, the sheer size of his bright red shoes as they flapped around below his barely three-foot frame. She knew him by reputation, but had never before seen him in person – this could only be Alfonzo, the shortest clown in all of France.

In an instant, she burned for him. His brightly painted face, his mismatched clothes, his trick lapel flower – oh, how she yearned to be squirted by that flower. How she longed to cradle that lopsided face in her hands, to kiss that shining red nose. Doubtless her colleagues would think her mad. After all, she was not only a renowned philosophical and religious thinker, but had been devoutly celibate for some twenty years now. She had even written a book dismissing circuses as a culturally bankrupt dead-end of the carnival tradition. To make things worse, she was violently allergic to straw, canvas and face paint, and had an irrational fear of trained animals of all kinds.

She hurriedly stuffed philosophical treatises into her desk and locked the lid with trembling hands. Her article on the dichotomy of free will would have to wait – she had no choice now but to run away and join the circus.

9

Mix metaphors.

Seeing the lie of the land and bracing for impact, I stepped up to the plate and prepared to eat my words. In the hollow blankness of the auditorium, my creaking cough thundered like a volcano going off, a single pistol shot in the echoing cavern of expectation before me.

'So,' I began, my throat as dry as my wit, which was as sharp as my tone, 'we seem to have reached a fork in the garden path you've been leading me up like a lamb to the slaughter. A turning point of no return, you might say.'

I hadn't expected this to be a groundbreaking barnstormer of a speech, but it was going down like the stock value of a lead balloon manufacturer. The silence that followed was as long as a freight train, as deep as a philosophy textbook and as uncomfortable as this analogy.

10

Cast children's stories exclusively with orphans.

Standing outside the rhinoceros enclosure, Billy tried to hide his distress from his friends. It was in just such an enclosure that his parents had died when he was barely four years old. He could still see the rhino's breath hanging in the cold air as they clung to one another in fear. Of course, they had actually died from the effects of the virulent plague they carried, passing away while the rhino was distracted by the arrival of a pair of unfortunate parachutists – his best friend Suzie's parents, as it turned out. They had been gored to death by the rhino while, in the sky far above, the plane they had jumped from exploded in mid-air, killing the pilot and co-pilot, who were Nate's mum and dad, respectively.

'You okay, Bill?' asked Suzie, laying a hand gently on his shoulder.

'Yeah,' replied Billy. 'Just … you know.'

'Yeah,' agreed Nate, looking wistfully at the clouds above them. Just then, Naomi came back from the toilets, grinning broadly.

'My parents should be here to pick us up soon,' she chirped happily. 'I love coming to the zoo.'

'Shut up, Naomi,' muttered Billy.

11

Have everything happen suddenly.

Suddenly, the bridge went deathly quiet. Then, just as suddenly, Mallone spoke.

'I'm suddenly not so sure,' he admitted, suddenly. Just as he was saying this, he caught a sudden movement out of the corner of his eye. He spun round just in time to see the sudden arrival of an unexpected figure. It was the captain, suddenly limping in with blood on his hands. Suddenly, Mallone understood what had happened.

'I feel suddenly ... cold ...' the captain suddenly whispered before suddenly collapsing. With quick, sudden movements of his expert but suddenly shaking hands, Mallone began to tend to his captain's wounds.

'You,' he suddenly barked, 'I need bandages and morphine. And make it sudden.' Before Mallone could suddenly save him, though, the captain was suddenly dying in his arms. Mallone suddenly leaned in to hear his sudden last words.

'Tell my wife ...' the captain suddenly rasped, his breathing suddenly urgent and sudden. 'Tell my wife ... I suddenly ... love her.'

12

Present your research in the form of dialogue.

'My god,' murmured Geoff. 'So it's true. We hold in our hands the original draft of the hitherto unknown third treaty of the 1648 Peace of Westphalia signed by the Holy Roman Emperor Ferdinand III himself.'

'Yes,' confirmed Sally. 'Who would have thought when we set off this morning for this remote Swiss village that we would end the day in possession of the very document which marked the birth of modern European state-hood?'

'Certainly not me!' laughed Geoff.

'Nor me!' Sally guffawed.

'And to think,' Geoff extemporised, 'the Ratification of the Treaty of Münster occurred exactly three hundred and sixty-one years ago last week!'

13

Commit to your genre.

With a manly flick of his muscular wrist, Captain Dash Gallant engaged the space drive and accelerated into the darkness of the Cloud Nebula. His destination was Mysterion IV, the uncharted planet which, as space-legend had it, was home to the quasi-mythical race of psychic aliens known as the Klar'Voyates.

He leaned back in his synthimesh podchair, the subtle tug of the starfighter's 0.8G inertia field holding his taut buttocks firmly on the nanobot-engineered cushion. Suddenly, his heroic concentration was shattered by the metallic keening of the ship's Sonic Audio Sound Alarm System (SASAS). He glared masculinely at the visiscan monitor and space-cursed under his breath at what he saw – a Mhal-Evol'Unt warship off the starside bow. Activating the subionic communication channel, he manfully barked an order to his inept yet adorable robot sidekick, Fumblebot.

'Prepare all weapons for an epic battle,' he gruffly intoned. 'And fire up the Annihilatatron-X.' He narrowed his steel-blue eyes, looking through the quantum-shielded plexipanel at the blackness of deep space. 'You never cease to amaze me, galaxy,' he whispered heterosexually.

14

Fail to contextualise dialogue.

He burst into the room.

'So it was you all along.'

'Yes, that's right.'

'You were behind the whole thing!'

'Not quite. You see, it was his idea.'

'Whose idea?'

'My idea.'

'You? But I thought you were ...'

'Not quite. You see —'

'No, let him answer for himself.'

'Where did you come from?'

'I was behind him.'

'Me?'

'No, the first one.'

'Me.'

'Hang on, which of you was the murderer? I've lost track.'

'I think it was him.'

'Was he the one who burst into the room, or was that you?'

'I think it was me.'

'Who spoke first?'

'How many of us are there?'

'One, two, three – and myself. I make it four.'

'What about her?'

'Oh, hi everyone. Have we found out who the murderer is yet?'

15

Pick the wrong hero.

Once upon a time, there was a king who was wise and strong and handsome and clever and all the people in the kingdom loved him. However, he had never found a wife. All women adored him, of course, but he was so devoted to ruling his kingdom wisely and enjoying all the wonderful food and wine his subjects produced – particularly the wine – that he had never found the time for marriage.

In order to make his kingdom the best it could be, he took a lot of money off his subjects in taxes, so it was important that he spent lots of money on wine so they would get some of those taxes back. He was a very thoughtful king. And in order to keep his kingdom safe, he executed a criminal every day and hung the dead body on the gate of his palace. Some days, the king's guards had to work very hard to find someone who looked like a criminal.

One day, the king was walking in the grounds of his palace when he saw a beautiful servant girl carrying two pails of milk to the kitchen. The king, being a romantic at heart, noticed that with her hands full, there was no way the servant girl could stop him touching her. And that, dear reader, is where our tale truly begins.

16

Use semicolons because you think they look good, not because you know how they work.

Then; as if by magic; the curtain fell and the entire theatre erupted into applause. I was of course delighted the reception was more than

I could have hoped for I felt pride swelling; in my chest. Turning to the director; I gushed; 'They love; me they really love; me!'

He winked; and motioned to the centre of the stage. I took my place and felt the whoosh of; hot air; as the curtain swept up again. Clap; clap; clap; clap; clap; clap; clap; clap. Went the crowd.

17

Explain the plot all at once.

With a low creak and the percussive rattle of hundreds of gears aligning at once, the airship shuddered into life.

'This is ...' breathed Timmy, his eyes widening. 'I had no idea.'

The Colonel grinned at him. 'You see, the vessel has a mind of its own,' he explained. 'Among Dr Edgar's many achievements was the invention of an artificial brain. He was the original owner of this magnificent machine and, incidentally, your real father.'

'My father ...' Timmy gasped in disbelief.

'Yes,' continued the Colonel, his eyes twinkling with new information. 'And his mind, his very essence, is contained in the valves and pistons of this airship, the key to which you have carried in your pocket all along.'

'But —' stuttered Timmy.

'Ssh,' the Colonel whispered. 'We don't have much time. I didn't mention this before so as not to worry you, but the world is in danger and you're the only one who can save us all.'

'I —' Timmy began.

'You are a direct descendent of King Arthur,' interrupted the Colonel, 'and I am a figment of your imagination. We are being chased by shadowy agents of a mysterious organisation and this airship is the only means of escape.'

'I understand.' Timmy nodded. 'I've got to fly the airship, which I know how to do because I'm a champion kite-flyer, which I forgot to mention before, but I am.'

'Exactly,' confirmed the Colonel. 'And the year is 1882.'

18

Write from multiple points of view within a single scene.

Arianna Milieux ran out onto the boulevard, her heart pounding ridiculously in her burning chest beneath her casual yet stylish clothing. The white-hot fire of love was combusting within her and she could feel her very soul literally yearning for Alfonzo with every step and stumble across the crowded pavement. She looked desperately around. How will I find him in this crowd? she thought in a panic. She was simply too far away from Alfonzo as he strode purposefully along the tree-lined thoroughfare, his ears full of the sound of cheering, his mouth moving silently as he repeated his own personal mantra to himself, his one concession to a secret anxiety that, unbeknown to his adoring public, tugged at his every thought – too far to even see him, let alone hold him as she longed to.

You are as tall as any man here, Alfonzo soundlessly whispered as he hopped nimbly over a pile of droppings left by an elephant whose main concern in life was to please his keeper, a cruel man whose life had been blighted by abandonment, his father having left the family when the keeper was young, ostensibly to join the navy, but admitting his true destination – the poppy fields of Afghanistan – to no-one, perhaps not even himself. The elephant gave a resigned sigh and loosened his bowels again, frustrating his keeper, who had been mentally planning his next meal, and causing Alfonzo to reflect on the uneasy truce between man and beast upon which the entire circus enterprise rested. This was not a subject that much concerned the bluebottle whose erratic progress towards the elephant's droppings – the weight of which the elephant was glad to be rid of – took it directly past the end of Arianna's nose. She swatted at it ineffectually and cursed under her breath as Alfonzo felt the first twinges of cramp in his left leg, which did not appreciate having to bear the weight of the rest of Alfonzo's body, the body about which Arianna could not stop thinking.

19

Make the most of formatting.

'So,' *she began*, peering suspiciously inside <u>the bag</u>. <u>'This is the merchandise we talked about?'</u>

The salesman nodded. 'That's <u>right</u>,' he **confirmed**. 'It's **all there.** *Every* **last bit.**'

'*And if I take it?' she asked.* 'What <u>then</u>?'

He **shrugged.** '<u>Then it's</u> *yours*,' he <u>assented</u>. 'What **happens after that** is up *to you.*'

She <u>scanned</u> his face *for clues*, but saw **nothing**. She *hesitated. What should she do?* There was <u>no</u> guarantee that what she **thought** was in the **bag** was actually *what was in the bag.* **BUT WAS THAT A CHANCE SHE COULD TAKE?** *So much rested on this.* <u>So much.</u>

'*And* you'll *be* discreet?' **she asked.**

He *smiled.* '*I AM THE SOUL OF DISCRETION*,' he whispered.

20

Base your characters on real people.

Penny – thirty-three, beautiful and neigh-bourly – was trying to hold back tears as she pegged out the washing, which she did every Tuesday and Friday at 6pm.

'Oh,' she sobbed quietly to herself, 'if only there was someone who could comfort me. I am so distraught, although I do a good job of hiding it and you'd have to be very attuned to the subtle details of my daily routine to realise.'

Just then, her husband, whose name isn't really important, came out of the house. Swinging his grotesque, muscly arms by his sides, he walked stupidly over to Penny.

'What's wrong?' he asked like an idiot. Penny dabbed at her hazel-brown (with flecks of green (although it would only be possible to tell from a distance with a good-quality telescope in the right lighting)) eyes with the hem of a summer dress, which, had she been wearing it, would have made her look like an angel as she took the bins out on Thursdays.

'Oh, nothing,' she murmured, her voice like a spring meadow. 'I just wish there was someone who could look after me better than you do. Someone who really cares for me. Someone with a comprehensive knowledge of optics and a good vantage point.'

21

If in doubt, initiate sex.

'Phew,' breathed Professor Benkin. 'It looks like the readings from the Bohm reactor are back at normal levels. That was a close one.'

'It certainly was,' purred Alex, stroking his

arm. 'But what should we do to pass the time before the lockdown ends?'

'I'm sure we'll think of something,' Professor Benkin grinned.

Twenty minutes later, the vault door juddered into motion and rose to reveal a group of hazard-suited figures.

'You took your time,' observed the professor, putting his socks back on.

The foremost figure pulled off her hazard helmet, releasing a cascade of luscious, chestnut-brown hair.

'We thought you might appreciate some ... time alone,' she smirked. 'The two of you are going to need all your energy for the journey back.'

'Why?' asked Alex.

'Oh,' she whispered, running her fingertips lightly over her Geiger counter, 'you'll find out.'

Three hours later, the scientists arrived back at their lab, only to find an unexpected visitor waiting for them.

'Professor Benkin, Dr Molloy,' declared the President. 'The Government of the United States wishes to show their gratitude for your heroic efforts.' He smiled seductively. 'In any way we can ...'

22

Use ... dramatic ... ellipses ...

With a screeching cacophony of mechanical discomfort, the plane dipped unevenly towards the runway and ...

... made contact with the tarmac. The rubber on the tyres instantly shredded, the exposed metal sending a shower of sparks directly towards the stricken aircraft's fuel tanks, which ...

... were of course safely sealed. The plane skidded along the runway, hurtling ever closer to the airport's observation tower ...

... which luckily was still half a mile away, this being a sizeable airport. Wide-eyed and soaked in sweat, the pilot gripped the controls in front of him and silently cursed ...

... his decision to wear thermal underwear and reuse the same pair of disposable contact lenses he had worn yesterday. Then, with the inevitability of a volcanic eruption, the plane ...

... came to a halt safely and every single one of its unfortunate passengers ...

... disembarked.

23

Write thinly veiled, self-aggrandising autobiographical fiction.

Joe Stockley paced the floor of his study and cursed under his breath. Dammit, he thought, why am I such a brilliant writer that no-one ever understands the depth and complexity of my work? It's almost as if I'm the only real person in the world and all the other people are just automatons! No, that can't be. Can it ...?

Just then, he was interrupted by the ringing of his top-of-the-range mobile phone, an astonishingly expensive device that would have been the envy of all his friends if they weren't all so fantastically rich as well.

'Hello?' he answered, his voice booming with a timbre that was capable of simultaneously charming his many admirers and intimidating any who dared oppose him.

'Hello Joe,' a mellifluous voice came floating back. 'It's your loving wife here.'

'Hello, my beautiful-beyond-compare, talented and intelligent wife,' chuckled Joe, his laughter reverberating around the expensive fixtures and fittings of his luxurious home.

24

Narrate every scene in a matter-of-fact tone, no matter how exciting.

At this point, the dragon, which was larger than a single-decker bus but smaller than an articulated lorry, breathed some fire out of its mouth – or, more properly, exhaled a mixture of flammable gas and liquid, which was ignited by a spark from a gland in its throat. This burned several people quite badly, although the knight who is the subject of our story remained largely unharmed.

Naturally, this incident caused a reaction of fear and surprise among the local population. It also caused a not insignificant amount of damage to property, which would take local residents many weeks to repair. Aside from this immediate inconvenience, the subsequent disruption caused by reconstruction efforts would also have an adverse effect on the local economy in the medium term. The knight then hit the dragon with his sword, killing it, which was probably for the best.

25

Always use a thesaurus.

She manipulated the garment in a cogitative mode.

'Hmm,' she vocalised. 'This attire is verifiably marvellous. From what material is it constituted?'

'From the most meritorious velveteen,' defined her interlocutor, simpering profusely.

'Indeed?' iterated the party of the first part. 'That is felicitous.'

'Additionally, this specified object has the property of being diminished in terms of its defining mercantile characteristic, and can thus be taken possession of for the quantity of merely a half-dozen currency units,' the retail employee informed.

'Exoneration?' supplicated the protagonist.

The commercial tertiary sector worker eye-balled her perspicaciously.

'I told you, it's five ninety-nine. Do you want it or not?'

26

Choose one character to bully.

'So it's settled. We head north.' Her hand resting lightly on the pommel of her sword, Saltar looked at each of her companions in turn. Pheos returned her gaze coolly, sparks of shadow flickering around his gloved hands. Gramble shrugged and hefted his axe from one compact, muscled shoulder to the other. 'No objections?' queried Saltar. 'Then we ride as soon as ...' She hesitated. 'Where's Dingleton?'

'Curse him!' muttered Gramble, looking around. 'Stupid wretched creature.'

For his part, Pheos smiled archly. 'I believe our diminutive friend is currently relieving himself,' he murmured, nodding towards a nearby bush.

'Sorry!' shouted the bush. 'Sorry! Hang on, I'm just ...' The bush rustled and Dingleton fell out, his trousers around his ankles. 'Wooaah!'

He tumbled head over heels down the muddy slope, his hands stuck in his belt as he tried desperately to pull his pants up.

'Dingleton!' snapped Saltar. 'Get up. We're heading north. Where did you tie up the horses?'

'Tie up?' echoed Dingleton, a baffled expression on his face. 'They were ... um ...'

'I'll murder him!' yelled Gramble, gripping his axe.

'At least tell me you picked up the bag with the holy amulet in it,' Saltar sighed.

'The thing about that ...' Dingleton began, before losing his balance and falling flat on his face.

'Why is he here again?' hissed Pheos.

'I don't know,' Dingleton moaned quietly to himself. 'I really don't know. I'm not equipped for this. It seems cruel even to have brought me. When you think about it —' Whatever he had been about to say, it was muffled by the bird faeces that fell into his mouth at that exact moment.

27

Signpost your twists.

Agent Sam Glowingly waved a hand at the tangled web of notes on the whiteboard.

'So,' he reiterated, 'we still have no idea who the killer is.'

'No,' admitted McSleet. 'Unless we can find someone in the monastery who's able to leap thirty feet off the ground, pass through a stained glass window without breaking it and kill his victim through the power of sheer terror.'

'Not your average monk,' observed Glowingly. 'In fact, it sounds more like one of the legendary fighting monks that reputedly inhabited this very monastery hundreds of years ago, but whose secrets have been lost for generations.'

'Aye,' agreed McSleet. 'But we need to find a real solution, not sit here chit-chatting about ancient history that has nothing to do with the case.'

'You're right,' nodded Glowingly, getting up from his chair and adjusting his pistol holster. 'We've got no time for idle talk about legends that neither of us has any reason to believe are even true, let alone relevant to our current investigation.' He consulted his notebook. 'Where next?' he asked.

'We need to interview more potential witnesses,' muttered McSleet, fishing a battered pack of cigarettes from his coat pocket. 'How about Brother Laurence, who's been studying the ancient manuscripts that sat undisturbed in the monastery vault for centuries and who has also, incidentally, been working out quite a lot recently?'

'Okay,' sighed Glowingly with a shrug. 'But I think we're wasting our time.'

28

Refuse to resolve mysteries.

As the train shuddered to a halt, I lifted myself from the seat and once again examined my ticket. The printed destination remained smudged beyond legibility.

'We haven't gone where we were going, you know,' whispered a voice from behind me. I whirled around. No-one. As I backed carefully out of the carriage, I felt my shoes pinching at my feet. I looked down.

'These aren't my shoes,' I muttered. As I had slept, someone must have changed them. But who, and to what purpose? Across the toe of each shoe was an inscription in a language I could not read – the same language, I quickly realised, that the menu in the disappearing café had been written in. If only I had known the proprietor's name. As I approached the train's door, I caught a shadow of my own reflection in the darkened window. I had an inexplicable bruise above my left eye in the exact shape of the Rorschach blot that had set me off on this journey to begin with. I looked closer. It was hard to tell, but it looked like my eyes were blue instead of brown. Also, upon closer inspection, I was now a woman. I blinked. It took only a fraction of a second, but in the space of that blink, I suddenly understood the nature of memory and realised that I would never die, or at least not in the sense that we understand it.

I wish I could explain to you, dear reader, where the train had taken me and what happened next, but for reasons I am unable to divulge, I must say no more. Farewell, my friends, farewell.

29

Make your villain genuinely evil.

Lord Plunderfall threw his head back and laughed.

'Bwa ha ha ha! Your attempts to escape only serve to amuse me.' He waved a hand towards the children. Armed guards appeared from the shadows.

'Why are you doing this?' asked Freddie.

'Why?' Lord Plunderfall replied. 'You ask me why? Well, the answer is quite simple. I seek to destroy the entire world because I am pure evil and wish nothing more than the death of all humanity. Bwa ha h—'

'Really?' interrupted Bertha. 'That's it? Because that seems a bit improbable.'

'Improbable?' thundered the dark figure, uncertainly.

'Yes,' confirmed Freddie. 'It's not all that convincing as a motive. I mean, if you destroy the entire world, where will you live?'

'I ...' Plunderfall hesitated. 'Never you mind. I am a force of pure malignancy and I shall tear apart the very—'

'And if you kill everyone in the world,' reasoned Bertha, 'where will you get your food from? Are you going to run your own farm? Is having a smallhold part of your masterplan?'

'I don't ...' He seemed to be sweating under his metal mask. 'That is ...'

Freddie shrugged. 'It just doesn't seem like you've thought it through, you know?'

'Exactly,' agreed Bertha. 'And while we're on the subject, I'm sure there's a more practical material you could have made that mask out of. I imagine the metal edges really chafe.'

30

Write outside your comfort zone.

Dr Henry Billingsworth was a Nobel Prize-winning theoretical physicist and all-round renaissance man. In the course of his long career, he had held subatomic particles in the palm of his hand, excavated lava from the centre of the Earth and invented a whole new mathematical function, which supplemented the old-fashioned plus, minus, multiply and divide to create an unheard-of fifth way of doing sums. At present, he was absorbed in his new experiment – observing evolution in fruit flies.

'Look,' he barked at his assistant, pointing to one of the flies. 'That one's evolving. Just round the legs, at the back. Can you see that?' His assistant nodded and made a note. Billingsworth grabbed the notepad from him. 'You've got to make notes more quickly –

look, it just evolved again and you nearly missed it.'

Sometimes Billingsworth thought he should just fire all his assistants and take care of everything himself, but there was simply too much work to be done. After all, if he spent all night in the lab, when would he find time to attend to his personal project, translating the novels of Shakespeare into Brazilian?

31

Let your characters explain themselves.

Aggie stared down at the police interview table.

'I'm embarrassed and quite scared,' she confessed.

The policeman nodded. 'I'm aware of that,' he replied. 'However, I'm not above using your fragile emotional state to get the information I need. You see, despite sympathising with you and, to be entirely honest, being quite attracted to you, I am very good at my job.'

'I've noticed that you're attracted to me,' admitted Aggie, looking up and half smiling.

He glanced away hurriedly.

'That's right,' he stammered. 'I'm nowhere near as subtle as I think I am.'

'Now I'm wondering how I can use this to my advantage,' she mused. 'It's not the sort

of thing I'd normally do, but this is a stress-
ful situation and there's room for these kind
of surprises in the way that I've been char-
acterised.'

Just then, the door burst open.

'Right!' shouted the slightly higher-ranking
policeman, storming into the room. 'I'm here
to break the tension and to alter the pace of
the scene, which seems to have stalled
somewhat.'

32

End with an unexpected moral.

Digory Dog closed the door of his tumble-down house behind him and sat down in his favourite chair.

'Thank goodness that's all over,' he sighed.

'It was quite an adventure,' squeaked Mousemouse. 'Let's do it again!'

'Oh, Mousemouse!' Digory Dog laughed. 'You always want more excitement, don't you?'

'More, more, more!' screamed Mousemouse, waving his little paws in the air. 'More adventures! More mysteries! More fun! I've got to have more! More!' He was shaking now, his little eyes wide and slightly bloodshot.

'Mousemouse!' Digory Dog snapped. 'Stop it!'

There was an awkward silence.

'Look,' sighed Digory. 'I think it's time you admitted you have a problem. This is getting out of hand.'

'I just love adventure,' muttered Mousemouse quietly.

'It's an addiction and you need to seek help,' explained Digory Dog. 'You're not just hurting yourself, you're hurting those around you.'

'I know,' whispered Mousemouse, covering his face with his paws. 'I know.' He was crying now, tiny mouse tears of remorse splashing onto the floor beneath him.

'Come here,' murmured Digory, hugging Mousemouse to him. 'It's going to be alright. You've taken an important first step today.'

33

Exclaim!

Each absorbed in their own silence, they gathered around the coffin! The pale grey light of morning slanted through the window and lay in a distorted square across the dark wooden surface!

'So!' began Peter! 'I'm glad we could all make it!'

'Of course!' mumbled Cassie, quietly! 'You think I'd stay away?!'

For a moment, no-one made a sound! The air conditioner hummed quietly! All eyes were on the coffin, long and dark in front of them! Peter seemed to be about to speak, but paused, then just shook his head! Michael took a step back!!

'It's time to go!' he whispered!

One by one, they turned and walked slowly to the door, each pausing before they left to glance, one final time, at the last home their father would ever know! Peter was the last!! He looked back into the room and nodded once, curtly, before letting the door close behind him with a click!!!

34

Recap the previous book.

Daniel Peridue, newly appointed captain of the guard after his heroics at the battle of Langathon where he had single-handedly held the main keep of the castle against a determined strike force of magically strengthened ape-men called Grathraks, felt uneasy.

It had been three months since the Southern Enchanters had broken the centuries-old treaty and launched their attack under cover of night, only to be foiled by the swift actions of Lothar Shiningheart, who had revealed himself to be the long-lost heir of Lord Langathon and thus fulfilled the Prophecy of the Protector, as passed down from generation to generation of Ingturon scholars and eventually into the teachings of Yath'l Cth'dang, last of the Ingturon, who had nobly sacrificed himself at the Mountains of Rehethihimah to save Lothar's life and grant him the mysterious power of the Ancient Ones.

Now everything was quiet. Too quiet.

'Are you thinking what I'm thinking?' he asked his companion. Remi Longshanks, the reformed thief whose skill with throwing knives had proved to be invaluable when he and Daniel had infiltrated the Enchanters' inner sanctum and stolen their magical hearthstone, thus severing the link that allowed them to command the Grathrak army, looked up.

'Don't know,' he replied. 'Were you thinking that peace has settled uneasily on these lands and that the dark shadow of the Old Magic still lurks somewhere far to the south, despite our success in repelling the specific threats that previously faced us?'

'Pretty much,' nodded Daniel.

35

Use onomatopoeia to make your writing pop.

Susie knocked – *thunk thunk thunk* – on the door. After a few moments it opened with a creeeaakk …

'Susie Thirskiss, I assume? Salutations,' hissed a lisping voice.

'Uh … I … Uh …' stu-uttered Susie. From inside the house, she could hear a metallic clanking clatter. 'I don't know if …' CLUNK '… I have the right …' CLUNK '… address,' she stammered.

The man behind the door coughed out a low, rasping laugh – *kakh kakh kakh* – and grinned. He waved a hand in front of him – swooosh!

'This address,' he purred, with a twinkle in his eye – blingadingading – 'is always the right address.'

Susie's heart had been beating fast – *badabump badabump* – but now it sank –

psheeeeeeew – as she realised – *ding*! – the horrible truth – RAAAAAAGH!

36

Use fate as a plot device.

'So,' George pontificated, settling back in his chair. 'Having seen all the candidates, what are your thoughts?'

Louise tapped her pen on the table.

'Well,' she mused, 'I thought Jules was a fairly good fit. Ingrid had the most impressive CV in terms of past experience. But I think we should go with David.'

George nodded. 'I'd be tempted to agree,' he agreed. 'Despite not really being suitable for the position or having any of the relevant qualifications, I think David's the right choice, mostly because it's his destiny.'

'Yes,' confirmed Louise, thoughtfully. 'He doesn't seem to know a lot about marketing per se, but getting this job would be the first step in his meteoric rise to power and eventual corruption in a personal plot arc that echoes, among other cultural touchstones, *Citizen Kane* and the fall of Lucifer.'

'I'd have to concur,' nodded George. 'He was bumbling and inarticulate in the interview, his CV is written on what looks like a paper hand-towel and he was unapologetically an hour late for his appointment, but I think he's the guy for the job.'

'What are you going to write on the form?'

'I'll just put "indefinable sense of narrative momentum".'

37

Burn through your plot.

Ben, who had grown up in foster care without any idea who his real parents were, or even if they were still alive, woke up early and had toast for breakfast. He had got dressed and was just about to leave for his job in the registry office, where he helped to bring order and certainty to other people's births, marriages and deaths, thus fulfilling an unacknowledged psychological need on his part, when he heard the letterbox rattle.

When he had read the letter, which contained the name and address of a woman who the investigating agency had deduced might be his birth mother, he went to the train station instead of going to work and set out on a journey to find this woman. As he travelled, he met various people and encountered various situations that made him remember details of his early life. It was poignant.

Finally, he arrived at the address and met the woman named in the letter and they talked at some length before it became clear that she couldn't be his mother after all. It's possible that he would never find what he was looking for but maybe, after all these years, the search itself was more important than the answers he might one day find.

38

Make it hard to distinguish between characters.

Christopher, head of molecular biology at ICSBS, was just coming to the end of a long day in the lab. He was about to hang up his goggles and go home when he heard a knock on the door. He looked up. It was his friend and colleague Chris, who, as the head of biological sciences with a particular interest in molecular research, was his immediate superior.

'Hi Chris,' greeted Christopher. 'I was just leaving.'

'Me too,' nodded Chris. 'As soon as I've found Christine. Have you seen her?'

'Christine? She was here earlier.' Christine, a molecular chemist with a head for biology, was one of Christopher's closest colleagues. 'Have you asked Christof?'

'Christof?' asked Chris. 'Is he the new guy?'

'Yes,' confirmed Christopher. 'He's heading up the biochemical molecular engineering division, which means Krissy might be heading for chemical bioengineering.'

'Doesn't she have more of a biomolecular chemistry background?'

'No,' replied Christopher. 'I think you're thinking of Krystal.'

39

Improve the online visibility of your fiction through the careful use of keywords.

Fighting for breath, Britney Bin Laden sprinted away from the collapsing building with all the speed of a get-rich-quick scheme or celebrity nipple slip. A massive explosion tore seductively through the virgin wall behind her, a wall that was eighteen years old and ready for fun.

Yikes, thought Britney, this is certainly exclusive breaking news that might well affect current stock prices. Just then, a truck carrying cheap pharmaceutical goods veered off the road, narrowly missing her. That could have killed me, thought Britney, her life flashing before her eyes like a free bootleg movie download. There are so many things I regret. I wish I had won top prizes at an online Euro-Casino, or talked to more singles in my area.

'Britney!' someone shouted. She squinted through the smoke. It was her friend and lover, Jesus Michael Jackson-Obama-Sextape. 'Are you okay?' he yelled, offering her coupon codes for genuine software downloads.

40

Write yourself into a corner.

The Mhal-Evol'Unt Chieftain flexed its serrated mandibles and activated the translation panel before speaking.

'Allow me describe now,' the digitised voice rasped. 'You trapped are completely.' It stalked across the cell, its claws scratching against the metal floor like nails on a blackboard. Captain Dash Gallant, renowned hero of the Battle of Tor'Sang, smiled grimly.

'Is that so?' he replied.

'Fully correct,' the translator burbled. 'Walls containing you diamond compound are. Also forcefields beyond, instant death causing. Communications impossible. Negotiation impossible. Weapons, ship, equipment destroyed. No knowledge of your presence here has Earth Fleet. Moments away, entire ship with neuropoison gas fills, to which us immune, you vulnerable. Death certainty. To Gallant, Tor'Sang butcher criminal, farewell.'

'For a cannibal lizard-insect space mutant, you say a hell of a goodbye,' muttered Dash. The translator made a barking sound that might have been a laugh before the Chieftain turned and left the cell.

Dash examined his surroundings. The thing was right – escape would be impossible. Even if, by some miracle, he managed to get out of the cell, there would be nowhere to go that wouldn't soon be flooded with deadly nerve gas. Beyond the warship, which had no escape pods, there was only the emptiness of fifty parsecs of space in every direction. His luck had finally run out, he realised. This was the end.

41

Write yourself out of a corner.

The sirens had started blaring as soon as the Chieftain had left the cell. A few moments after that, tendrils of thick green gas had begun to snake under the door. However, Dash was aware of none of this. As soon as the door had closed behind his captor, he had begun the mental and physical process needed to put himself into the Trance of All-Being, an ancient secret taught to him by his mysterious Space-Zen master on the hidden ice planet of Bhulfhughugt. This trance would free him from the necessity of breathing, instead allowing him to re-metabolise the oxygen within his body for up to an hour.

Next, he formed a vivid mental image of his fifth birthday, a process that generated the unique combination of brainwaves required to activate the bio-integrated quantum communications implant that nestled deep in his hypothalamus. The nanotech circuitry instantaneously sent a burst of coded data tunnelling through non-space to the paired receiving unit, fifty parsecs away. Now he had broadcast his position, help was on its way.

That just left the diamond compound walls and deadly forcefields beyond. Taking a moment to channel the never-adequately-explained power of his Space-Zen abilities, Dash sensed a complex, syncopated rhythm in the electromagnetic fields that permeated the cell. He placed one hand against the wall and breathed for a moment. Then, guided by the fluctuations of unseen forces, he rapped a seemingly random pattern with his fingertips. For a split second, the crystalline structures within the wall aligned perfectly with the pulsing of the forcefield, reflecting and focusing its power in such a way as to not only overload the field generators, but vaporise the wall itself. With a shower of sparks and a crackle of exploding neutrons, the cell was gone.

Dash sprinted down the corridor, deadly neurotoxin gas swirling around him. The door to the ship's bridge opened as he approached. He combat-rolled through it. At the exact moment that he tumbled into the command centre, thirty heavily armed Mhal-Evol'Unt warriors turning to face him, an explosion rocked the ship. Through the plumes of smoke and a newly torn gash in the ship's hull, Dash saw the familiar figure of Fumblebot, his adorable robot sidekick.

'Well, gentlemen, this is my ride.' He laughed, waving one hand at his alien captors as he hurled himself through the haze of molten metal and into the waiting starfighter. With a whistle of friendly greeting, Fumblebot fired up the engines and they were away.

42

Use quotation marks for no apparent reason.

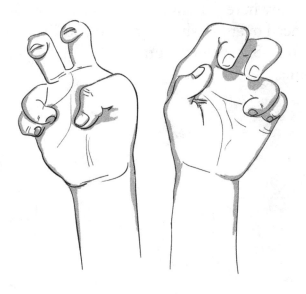

The sun was just 'setting' when I arrived home. The smell of 'bread' and the sound of 'laughter' drifted across the field. Already, the stresses of the day seemed like a 'distant memory.' I ran the last few yards, then rapped my fist against the 'door' and stepped into the kitchen.

'I'm home,' I sighed, partly to myself and partly to 'Mary.'

She turned to look at me, a 'smile' lighting up her 'face.'

'You were gone so long,' she cooed, giving me a 'hug'. 'I was getting "worried". Where were you?'

'"Nowhere."' I smiled. '"Nowhere" at all.' I glanced over her shoulder. 'Are you "baking"?'

'Yes.' She smiled. 'I'm really "glad" you're home.'

43

Describe the wrong things.

Carol stands absolutely still. In front of her,

not more than ten feet away, is a fully grown black bear. The ferns beneath its feet are crumpled and slightly browning, their delicate fronds pressed into the thick, wet mud of the forest floor. Carol hesitates. Slowly, very slowly, she looks around for a possible escape route. The light falling through the canopy of leaves has a pale, thin quality to it and the air is brackish with a faint scent of the stagnant water from the nearby estuary.

She decides to make a dash for it. Her shoes are slightly too tight, pinching at her toes and digging into the soft skin just above her heels. If she had put on thicker socks this morning, this wouldn't be a problem, but in her haste to leave the house, she had grabbed a thin white cotton pair designed to sit low on the ankle, hidden below the line of the shoe. Seeing her move, the bear leaps forward. A plane is flying directly overhead and the sound of its engines is like the rumble of a distant washing machine. It is a passenger plane of some sort – most probably an old 737 with a good few years of service still ahead of it.

The bear eats Carol.

44

Censor your characters.

'I've been a docker for twenty stinking years and now you're telling me I'm out of a job because of these flipping cutbacks?' Eddie clenched his fists. 'Well, you can go forget yourself! I'm blinking angry about this!'

'For fudge's sake, Eddie, calm down,' snapped his supervisor, spreading his hands in a soothing gesture. 'It's not my decision. It's those blinking numbskulls in management who've come up with this frolicking plan.'

'Yeah?' muttered Eddie. 'Well, they're out of their damp minds. I ought to go up there and smash their flaking heads in.'

'I talked to them already, Ed. They say they can't change the situation.'

'Can't?' exploded Eddie. 'They can't? That's what they always say. It's can't this and can't that and can't the other. If you ask me, they're a bunch of—'

'Eddie,' his supervisor interrupted. 'I need you to flapping cool it right flouncing now.'

45

Be clear about what objects can and can't do.

The socks he had on were thick and woollen and he knew they would keep his feet warm, but they could never insulate his soul against the chill of guilt. He rubbed his hands together briskly and breathed out a cloud of warm breath – a cloud that was neither large nor opaque enough to hide his face from the judgement of the world. Then, sheltering from the wind that could not blow away his troubles, he dug in his pocket – a pocket too shallow to contain all the secrets he carried with him – and pulled out a roll of mints. It took him a few attempts to unwrap them, just as it had taken him a few attempts to leave the house – but this time because his fingers were numb with the night's cold, a physical numbness that had no bearing on his (also numb) emotional state. His hand shaking – a simple physical reaction to temperature rather than a sign of the fear he felt – he put a mint in his mouth. Its refreshing taste made his tongue tingle with sensation, but it could not prompt a similar feeling in his life as a whole, which remained torpid and unrefreshed by the cooling spearmint flavour of the powdery tablet.

46

Drop in and out of reported dialogue for no clear reason.

'So, what'll it be?'

By the way the captain was looking at me and idly hefting his cutlass, I could tell that he had a fate in mind for me already.

'Will ye be joining us, or ...?'

'I, uh ...' The edge of the cutlass was glinting in the firelight. 'Tell me again where you're headed,' I asked.

He replied, telling me the crew's planned itinerary for the next few months and mentioning various likely events along the way, which he presumably thought would entice me into a life of piracy. I had to admit, there were appealing elements.

'I have to admit,' I admitted, 'there are appealing elements.'

He reminded me of my current precarious status as a guest aboard his ship, using turns of phrase that, while not precisely threatening, did little to reassure me as to my continued safety as a non-crew member aboard the *Pewter Squid*. I answered in such a way as to try to play for time, but he interrupted me with some evident frustration. I attempted to placate him. He pressed me for a firm commitment. I acceded.

'Grarrr,' he roared. 'A fine decision, lad.' He followed this with more warm words, telling me that one day I would captain my own ship and that I would find him a fair and equitable leader provided I never crossed him. 'Provided ye never cross me,' he concluded.

'I assure you,' I assured him – the rest of the sentence I spoke was the substance of my assurance, which was the promise that I would never betray his trust.

'Glad ...' he chuckled; the concluding part of this sentiment confirmed that what he was glad about was 'to hear it'.

And that, dear friends, is how I began my career as a pirate and syntactic grammarian.

47

Use very specific reference points in your similes.

Digory Dog gasped. The man standing before them was the closest thing to a giant he had ever seen. He was as tall as the birch tree at the bottom of the garden at 64 Kenton Street, Ruislip, West London, and as wide as the bonnet of a 1989 Ford Festiva.

'Explain yourself!' thundered the giant, his voice as loud as the maximum volume setting on a Sony Trinitron KV-32S42 when tuned to white noise. 'What are you creatures doing in my kingdom?'

'Please sir,' stammered Digory Dog, as nervous as Dave Anglesey of New Park Road, Melbourne, while waiting for his biopsy results at eight thirty on a Wednesday morning, 'we didn't mean to trespass, really we didn't. It's just that your castle is as strange and fascinating as the first and, to a lesser extent, second seasons of the cult early nineties US television drama *Twin Peaks*, although, to be fair, it lacks the consistently compelling quality and fractured narrative of that well-loved landmark in television history.'

48

When writing radio drama, use
dialogue to set the scene.

ALBERT: Hullo? Who's there?

MEREDITH: I can see a light outside, Albert.

ALBERT: Yes, Meredith, I see it also. But what the devil —

F/X: A LOUD CRASH.

PETER: Aha!

ALBERT: My God, Meredith! It's Peter, your husband!

MEREDITH: Peter! What are you doing bursting suddenly into the room with a gun in your hand and a look of fury on your face?

PETER: I'm furious, Meredith. In fact, I'm pointing this gun at you right now.

ALBERT: Don't worry, Meredith, I'll wrestle him to the ground.

F/X: A TUSTLE.

MEREDITH: You're fighting him, Albert!

ALBERT: Yes, and I'm winning, too.
PETER: You have your foot on my windpipe and you are overpowering me.

49

Romanticise places.

I still remember the unique smell of Longlake, a gentle musk that carried on the breeze and wrapped itself around you like a comfortable old coat. It blew down from the power station on the hill, swooping over the rendering plant and through the sewage works before bringing its complex odour to the main street and the children's playground.

Ah, the playground. Many happy hours I spent in that glorious fenced-off paradise, digging through the damp woodchips beneath my feet and searching for treasure – a glinting shard of broken glass here, a mysterious hypodermic needle there. I still remember the time I found a strange-shaped balloon with a tiny reservoir of cloudy liquid in it. That was what Longlake was like – full of mystery and hidden wonder, from the burnt-out warehouse on the edge of town to the constant screech of brakes and occasional crunches of impact that came from the section of road the locals called 'decapitation corner'.

How I long to go back there, even now. They tell me that the sinkhole swallowed everything from the pawn shop to the prison, but maybe one day I'll head back to ol' Longlake, just to see.

50

Fail to notice are missing during editing.

As the of battle died down and twilight fell over the fields of Langathon, Lothar stood atop the hill and watched.

'So many have died here today,' he to his squire. 'Loyal to the last, every of them.'

'Sir,' muttered young man.

Lothar shifted his weight and leaned on the pommel his sword. He knew what meant – one day soon, he would king. There would be more battles like this, but none as bloody or as. The path was clear now, knew. He took a breath and raised his so that all men might hear.

'We emerge from victorious!' he bellowed. A ragged cheer came from the below. 'With the blood of our fallen friends still upon us,' continued, 'with the smell our enemies' fear in nostrils, with swords unsheathed and, we ride!' Another cheer rang the valley. 'We ride to Crown Point and to !'

51

Write as therapy.

Julie marched into the office and slammed her bag down on the desk.

'Right,' she barked. 'There are going to be some changes around here now I'm in charge.'

Everyone looked up, surprised by the new authoritative tone in Julie's voice and suddenly reassessing their view of her as a pushover who never stands up for herself.

'What do you mean, changes?' stammered Gordon, who now regretted ever having belittled Julie in front of that temp she liked despite her definitely telling him that she was going to ask him out.

'For a start,' declared Julie, her voice pulsing with purposeful mastery and newfound confidence, 'there'll be no more talking about TV shows from the night before that I haven't watched, okay?'

'Okay,' conceded José, the quiet and brooding but devastatingly handsome accounts manager. 'It is really annoying when we do that and it makes you feel left out, which isn't fair. Also, I love you and you're not getting too old to have children and your mother doesn't know what she's talking about because, if anything, your career is going from strength to strength.'

'Thank you, José,' smiled Julie, modestly.

52

Qualify every description.

Arianna stumbled blindly through the crowd on the boulevard in Paris in France, desperately searching for Alfonzo with her eyes. The intensely charismatic dwarf was nowhere to be found by a person looking for him in an attempt to find him, such as herself.

'Alfonzo!' she cried out with her voice from her mouth in her face. All she could hear with her sense of hearing was the clamour of the crowd, constituted of the noise they were making. Then, all of a sudden, the crowd – made up of all the people in the boulevard, which was lined by trees, the leaves of which were glowing in the bright afternoon sun – parted and she caught a visual glimpse with her eyes of the clown she lovingly adored with her feelings.

Before she could physically run to him with her legs and feet, though, she saw something that stopped her in her tracks, which she had been figuratively making by walking on the pavement, but which she was not making (either figuratively or literally) any more, since she had stopped. Alfonzo was using his arms and hands to cradle a person who was a woman who was a bearded lady from the same circus troupe of which Alfonzo was also a part in his capacity as a performer being, as he was, a clown. She watched as Alfonzo's hands on the ends of his arms snaked up the bearded interloper's back, caressing her like a seahorse caresses his young after carrying them for their two- to four-week gestation period, because it's male seahorses that get pregnant, not female ones.

She choked back liquid tears of water as he stroked the harlot's long, luxurious beard on her face. How Arianna wished in her mind that it was her beard he was stroking. Of course, she did not have a hair beard, being a professor of theology rather than a circus performer in a circus. But he could stroke her other bodily hair on her body, couldn't he? Her sensibly bobbed brown locks on her head, her barely visible downy upper-lip hair on her upper lip, the wispy tufts in her armpits under her arms and finally – she barely dared imagine with her imagination – her delicate and mysterious hoo-ha. Just thinking the word gave her a thrill. It had an earthy sensuality to it, a deep and primal power that spoke to the very fabric of her nature. Hoo-ha. She trembled silently, without making a noise. Hoo-ha.

53

Don't not use double negatives.

Although I wasn't unfamiliar with the failings of post-structuralism, this particular book lacked some of the omissions I didn't expect to not find. I had neglected to read the index, but this was an oversight that failed to concern me – that is to say, if I hadn't neglected the index, my lack of neglect wouldn't have concerned me less.

'This doesn't fail to be a non-trivial problem,' I muttered to myself. 'There couldn't be the absence of something I'm failing to miss, could there?'

It wasn't something other than nonsense to imagine that I'd succeeded in failing to untangle the many far from non-linguistic problems that this text certainly didn't lack. I just didn't seem to be able to identify the missing elements – or rather, the absence of them. Perhaps my failure to find those omissions was itself not insignificant.

'Maybe I'm being too negative,' I didn't not whisper to no-one other than myself.

54

Have your characters see themselves in mirrors.

Joe Stockley gave himself a wry grin as he passed the full-length mirror in the hallway. He was a striking figure, well clear of six foot in height and made to seem even taller by the exquisitely tailored morning suit he had thrown on effortlessly yet perfectly that morning. His eyes twinkled with the playful intelligence of cynical wisdom that informed his every action. The grin he gave himself was one of quiet recognition rather than vanity, for self-regard was a vice he had studiously avoided in his quest for perfection.

Meanwhile, Joe's wife, Angelica, waited for him patiently at their regular restaurant table, idly turning a highly polished spoon over and over in her hands. As the light flashed off it, she caught a glimpse of her own face, breath-takingly beautiful even with the distorted reflection the curved surface of the spoon offered her. Her deep brown eyes shone with the light of compassion, which had emanated from her for as long as anyone could remember, bathing all who met her in the glow of her kindness and love. With the slightest motion of her hand, she called over a waiter.

Antonio, who had been admiring Angelica from a discreet distance, did his best to glide effortlessly as he approached the table. Looking up, he met his customer's eyes and was about to speak when he saw himself reflected in their soft radiance. He was in his late thirties, athletic in build and outwardly self-assured. The slight creases around his eyes betrayed a lifetime of both tears and laughter. Reflected in them, he could faintly make out the darkened window of the restaurant, which in turn reflected an image of himself standing at the table holding his notepad and highly polished pen. In fact, so highly polished was the pen ...

55

If you find a phrase you like, keep repeating it.

Needless to say, I was fully aware of the behind-the-scenes machinations which, needless to say, would ultimately result in my departure from the executive board of VoxMagic Enterprises. The VP of Product Interface Experience who was, needless to say, a close personal friend of mine, kept me fully informed of who was saying what to whom and when – needless to say, this involved me needlessly hearing a lot of what people had to say about me, which, needless to say, was not all of a positive nature.

Needless to say, this period of needless naysaying was brought to a swift (although, needless to say, temporary) end by the introduction of our revolutionary predictive transcription system, VoxMagic Ultra, which, needless to say, changed the whole face of voice-recognition technology, allowing, as it did, the pre-emptive conversion of spoken words to text. Needless to say, it was an exciting time for the whole industry, no matter what anyone might needlessly say about the needs of, say, the consumer and, it needs to be said, I was at the forefront of this (needless to say) revolutionary paradigm shift. For the first time, we had produced speech-recognition software so advanced that we had eliminated the need to actually say anything.

56

Create subplots that bear no relation to the main story.

Meanwhile, the ant whose escape from the sugar bowl had been witnessed by Mary at the pre-wedding dinner was struggling to return the sugar he had collected to his colony. Everywhere he turned, his path was blocked by puddles, the same puddles that had previously dampened the hem of Lisa's wedding dress, although of course the ant didn't know anything about that, being not only peripheral to proceedings and not an official guest at the function, but an ant.

Elsewhere, the builder who had been sub-contracted to remodel the stables of the stately home in which Lisa's wedding was taking place was preparing to tuck into a well-earned packed lunch. Being on the other side of the estate from the wedding party, he was unaware that the ham he had in his sandwiches was roughly the same colour as the centre of the chicken breasts currently being served to the wedding guests and would remain unaware of the events unfolding in the dining hall even as several aunts hurled and retched into the dahlias.

57

Describe characters in minute detail, taking no account of narrative pacing.

Secret Agent Sam Glowingly glared at the precipice in front of him with his rich, soft brown eyes – a kind of mahogany chocolate colour flecked with the faintest hint of jade green.

'Damn,' he snarled, his voice attaining a timbre at once harsh and resonant, like a slightly damaged cello. He knew he would never survive the drop to the foliage below, and the demonic monk would be upon him at any moment. If only McSleet had survived the explosion at the warehouse – McSleet, with his rough, slightly smaller than average hands – together, the two of them might have had a chance. Glowingly glanced over his gently sloping shoulder and saw the wiry, muscled, angular and gaunt figure of the monk emerge from the tunnel behind him. Without hesitation, he planted his narrow size eleven feet firmly on the ground and leaped out into the void.

As he felt his weight – the weight that had been steadily increasing for the last ten years and showed no sign of diminishing, at least while his sister Marie continued to excel as she did at the design and production of delectable gourmet meat pies – pulling him down into the valley below, he spread his subtly out-of-proportion arms and clenched his square, compact fists. The wind whipped through his medium-length sandy brown hair, which tended towards a dryness he found frustrating and did his best to remedy by using a range of haircare products advertised by the supermarket as 'nourishing', but which he had never felt made much of a difference, and the ground hurtled rapidly towards him.

58

Include unnecessary linguistic redundancies of language.

Kevin entered his PIN number into the ATM machine at a rapid rate of speed. He had a preplanned date arrangement with a female woman and didn't want to be delayed by lateness. If he compared and contrasted Olivia with previous girlfriends he'd dated before, she was universally superior and better in every way. He grasped and took his card from the mechanical machine.

'Hurry quickly,' he whispered under his breath, his hand advancing forward towards the cash slot where his money would come out. He glanced at the LCD display, which was showing an advertising commercial. 'I'm in too much of a rush to have time for this,' he muttered. 'You can keep your added bonus free gift.'

Finally at last, his cash money emerged into view and he grabbed it with his hand.

Irregardless of this delay, the end result of his date arrangement would be a new beginning at this moment in time. Little did he know or realise, but his goals and objectives were about to be completely and utterly met in a way and manner it was impossible to overexaggerate.

59

Personify every object.

The hat, old and disillusioned, sat on my head like a passenger on a bus that is not only late, but has forgotten which route it was supposed to be taking. The feather drooping pathetic-ally from the hat's side seemed to have given up any hope of escape and was now, to all intents and purposes, playing dead. I shuffled my shoes, which were not having the best day, on the gravel; first the chewing gum they had picked up two miles back and now this. As for the chewing gum, it was just disappointed to be stuck to a pair of shoes with such a low tolerance for discomfort.

My grimy, tactless finger hovered hesitantly over the unsuspecting doorbell for a second before pushing it. The sound of the chimes filled the inside of the house like a sumo wrestler in a minicab before dying away like a sumo wrestler on life support. The silence that followed outstayed its welcome like a guest at a party that didn't want to be thrown, much like a javelin entertaining thoughts of retirement in a country cottage that sits contentedly on a hilltop that reaches for the clouds like a dieter for cream cakes that wish they didn't have to be eaten.

60

Beat around the bush.

The doctor tapped his pen on his clipboard and coughed.

'Well, Mr Wolfowitz,' he began, 'you suffer from a rare disorder known as Chronic Recurrent Meta-Synodic Genetic Reconfiguration.'

'Okay,' growled Art, scratching the back of his hand. 'What does that mean?'

'Let me put it like this,' the doctor explained. 'The episodes you have described experiencing and the associated symptoms – chronic restlessness, argyrophobia, sudden, unexplained hair growth, uncontrollable aggression – seem to occur on a regular cycle, do they not?'

Art nodded and flexed his toes, which suddenly felt very restricted inside his shoes. 'What's your point?' he barked.

'That cycle is, broadly speaking, monthly, is it not?' asked the doctor.

'Yeah. So?' Now his ears itched. He scratched at them.

'And the episodes only occur at night, is that correct? When the moon is visible?'

'Look,' snarled Art. 'What are you getting at?' He was feeling irritable and, all of a sudden, hungry.

'The truth is, Mr Wolfowitz,' the doctor sighed, 'very little is known about Chronic Recurrent Meta-Synodic Genetic Reconfiguration. I'd like to keep you in overnight for tests. You can sleep here, in this flimsily-built cage, just underneath the skylight.'

61

Risk the narrator's life.

As I dangled from the precipice, I felt absolutely certain that I would die. My fingers were slipping slowly but inevitably from the ledge and with no-one else for a hundred miles in every direction, I knew for a fact that there was no hope of rescue. In fact – and I don't mind telling you this now, in the warmth and comfort of my own home – I had fully accepted the fact of my own death even before I lost my grip and went hurtling into the abyss below.

As dictated by cliché, the entirety of my life unfolded in my mind's eye, from birth through childhood to early adulthood and finally to this, my final, fatal misadventure. As I tumbled through the air towards absolutely certain death with no hope of a reprieve, I found a strange kind of peace. I knew beyond a shadow of a doubt that my days were at an end – to the extent that if by some highly un-likely miracle I was to survive, it would be so unfeasible as to be virtually an insult to any hypothetical audience who might be ob-serving me. I was a goner and I knew it.

Before I continue my story, may I refresh your glass? Are you quite comfortable enough? Excellent. Now, on with the tale …

62

Refuse to give names to characters.

A tall man with glinting eyes stepped mean-ingfully from the ship's gangplank and surveyed the dock.

'Where is she?' he demanded, gesturing at a stooped and subservient man beside him.

'Sorry, sir?' the servile man asked. The tall man with the smooth black walking stick clicked his tongue impatiently.

'You know who,' he snapped. 'The demure woman with the scarf.'

'I'll make enquiries, sir,' the balding, dimin-utive man replied (the same man who had been talking a moment before).

'Well, make them quickly,' interrupted a tall man with shining eyes. This was not the same tall man with glinting eyes who had so far been conducting the conversation, but a new, even taller man with eyes that shone rather than glinted, who had just disembarked behind the two figures already standing on the dock.

'You!' hissed the tall (merely tall – not taller) man with glinting rather than shining eyes. 'I should have known you would try to interfere.'

'Interfere?' queried the tallest available man with the really quite unsettlingly shiny eyes. 'I would never interfere. I am merely concerned for our mutual acquaintance's wellbeing.'

'The demure woman?' asked the second-tallest man.

'I would describe her as more reserved than demure.'

'Ah.' The still-actually-quite-tall-though-short-comparatively-speaking man replied. 'I'm not entirely convinced we're talking about the same woman.'

63

Get fixated on a particular reference
point.

Geoff craned his neck and looked up at the
building.

'Soon they'll be everywhere,' he muttered.
'Pinkman and Grist Associates, sweeping
across the financial district like Genghis Khan,
destroying everything in their path.'

'Not if we stop them,' replied Felicity,
quietly.

Geoff shook his head. 'We're like unarmed
Chinese peasants,' he sighed. 'They'll run us
down on horseback.'

'But the antitrust investigation —' began
Felicity.

'Useless,' Geoff interrupted. 'Like a bamboo
hut. They'll lie to the regulators, they'll lie to
the courts, they'll do whatever it takes and
come out clutching the still-beating heart of
the bonds market like a newborn Genghis

Khan emerging from his mother's womb clutching a bloodclot – a story that, whether apocryphal or not, indicated the high regard in which Genghis Khan's capacity for bloodthirstiness was held by his people.'

'I know,' nodded Felicity. 'That's what you always say.' She stared down at her shoes, made of the same kind of leather as Genghis Khan's saddle would once have been.

Geoff's gaze was still on the skyscraper above them. 'How tall would you say it is?' he mused. 'If you got two hundred Genghis Khans and stood them on each other's shoulders ...'

64

Underestimate your audience.

Arianna slammed the apartment door behind her and collapsed onto her divan, which is a kind of chair. She covered her face with her hands – something that people do when they are upset – and closed her eyes. *How could I have been so stupid?* she thought to herself, even though she already knew the answer (this is called a rhetorical question). The man she loved was with someone else, which is a situation that tends to make people sad. She was sad.

What good is all of this, she thought, looking round the luxurious apartment, *if I can't be with him?* Again, this was a rhetorical question, because she thought that her home and possessions were no good if she couldn't be with Alfonzo. Also, 'luxurious' means very comfortable and expensive and an apartment is a set of rooms in a large building that you can live in. She couldn't think about anything but Alfonzo (but she probably could have done if she really needed to, like if the building was on fire or a wolf was attacking her) when she closed her eyes; all she could see was the image of him cradling the bearded lady who had stolen his heart (1. She could see this in her imagination, not in real life, although it had happened in real life; 2. Alfonzo's heart had not literally been stolen – this is a metaphor; 2(a). 'literally' means exactly, in reality; 2(b). a metaphor is when you describe something as if it was something else to try to explain it).

65

Give every character a tragic backstory.

Rape victim Laura Nuffield examined the tiles on her rack. The triple-word score seemed out of reach for now, but maybe if she ...

'Come on, come on,' barked Pete, who had lost an eye in the same childhood accident that had killed his twin brother. 'We haven't got all day.'

'Oh Pete,' laughed Andrea, whose crippling bouts of depression had led her more than once to the brink of suicide. 'Leave Laura alone. It's only a game.'

'Yeah, Pete,' agreed Simon. 'You took long enough on your turn.' He flashed Pete the sympathetic smile that had been his trademark since he had escaped from the religious cult that had indoctrinated him, taken all his money and forced him never to see his family again.

'I'm sorry,' Pete apologised, bravely struggling with his lack of adequate depth perception, 'but I've got a real doozy lined up here.'

'Lucky you,' grumbled Laura. 'The only word I can make is "pain", and I can't find a place to put it.'

'How about there?' pointed Andrea, with a chuckle. 'Using the "A" from "anguish"?'

66

Subtly weave your own opinions into
the narrative.

Simone was late home from work that day,
something that could have been prevented had
the council consulted more widely before im-
plementing their scheme to fully pedestrianise
the city centre. At the moment her key turned
in the lock of her front door, it was 6:36pm and
the streetlights, despite the fact it had been
getting dark for the last hour, were just beginning to blink on (another result of the local
authority being in the pocket of environment-
al pressure groups).

At first, she didn't see the body slumped in
the middle of her living room, bleeding onto
the carpet and making stains which would
undoubtedly require the use of a cleaning
product the sale of which was restricted due to
its 'hazardous' chemical content. In this situation, it seemed, the need for effective carpet

shampoo would be forgotten in the mindless rush to protect every so-called endangered fish in every scummy pond. She screamed in terror, producing a noise which in all likelihood would be described as 'noise pollution' by some faceless bureaucrat who thinks he can tell us all what to think. Her hands trembling, she reached for her phone (the phone which, if the green thought police had their way, she wouldn't even be able to charge up except by putting an unsightly wind turbine in her own back garden) and dialled the emergency number.

'Hello?' she gasped, using up a small amount of oxygen, which probably made her a bad person according to the maniacs who think we should all worship trees and go around singing lullabies to flowers. 'I need the police here right away.' She listened to the operator for a second, although you're probably supposed to call them telephonically challenged equal-opportunity non-gender-specific secular emergency operatives these days. 'Okay. Well, how long will it take them on bicycles?'

67

Solve mysteries by introducing more mysteries.

'So the vault was never broken into at all?' asked Mr Hain, his brow furrowed in confusion.

'Correct,' chuckled Caldwell. 'But someone did get inside.' He paused, giving the gathered company a moment to catch up with his dazzling mental acuity.

'An inside job?' Mr Hain gasped. 'At my bank?'

Caldwell turned to him and smiled. 'You could say that.' He raised one gloved hand and pointed to the bank manager's head. 'Would you please remove your hat?' Slowly, Mr Hain lifted his black bowler. 'And would you kindly look inside?'

'My god,' gasped Mr Hain, staring in disbelief at the lining of his hat.

'That, ladies and gentlemen,' explained Caldwell, with a small flourish of his hand, 'is an occult inscription placed in our good friend Mr Hain's headwear in order to control his every thought and action.'

'Placed there?' whispered Lady Petunia, her voice trembling. 'But by whom?'

'Whom indeed,' mused Caldwell. 'Someone with considerable knowledge of mysterious black arts. Someone with access to Mr Hain's hat. Someone able to perform such an act and go completely undetected.' He paused, listened intently and took one step to his left before swinging his arm wildly in the air.

'Gaaah!' yelled a voice, seemingly from nowhere. Caldwell grabbed at thin air and shook his fist. 'Alright, alright,' grumbled the voice. 'You can stop it now.'

With a shimmer of pale light, a figure appeared, Caldwell's hand gripping its cravat.

'This,' revealed Caldwell, 'is Mr Laender, a demon of considerable power.'

'A demon?' gasped Lady Petunia.

'Yes, my lady,' confirmed Caldwell. 'A demon summoned and solicited by you, a time traveller from the future.'

'Curse you!' screamed Lady Petunia, peeling her synthetic face off and revealing the hyper-intelligent lizard beneath. 'Curse you to the seventeen dimensions of hell!'

For a moment, the assembled company – detective, bank workers, policemen, demon and time-travelling lizard – were silent.

'Um,' mumbled Mr Hain, tapping his fingers on the edge of his hat. 'I mean ... Are you absolutely sure it wasn't just a break-in?'

68

Get as much detail into your opening sentence as possible.

No more than three feet away from Julius (but certainly more than two feet away; perhaps thirty inches – or, in the system preferred by Helen, Julian's wife, of whom more later, seventy-six point two centimetres – although needless to say, it seemed less) a dog that seemed to be a cross between a doberman and some kind of beagle – its appearance certainly seemed to fit the original meaning of the Old French word 'begueule' (literally, open-mouthed) from which 'beagle' is derived – was barking in the key of E-flat and pawing the air in a way that, had there been an invisible miniature piano beneath its claws, might have produced a melody not dissimilar to a free jazz composition of the early sixties or, more likely, a discordant jumble of sharps and flats that, had this been the case rather than being merely a fanciful possibility (which is what it was), would have put Julius's teeth on edge in a way that the dog's barking, in the absence of the more musical set of noises just touched upon, was already managing to do.

69

Learn about syllepsis, then refuse to stop employing it.

Joe Stockley was in an expensive sports car and deep trouble. This time, he had really let his mouth and his exotic foreign lover run away with him and it was getting beyond a joke and his immediate circle of friends in the form of rumours and speculation.

As he ran a red light, the conversation back in his mind and away from his troubles, he couldn't help but feel a sense of rising panic and the soft matte finish of his hand-stitched leather steering wheel. Angelica had been absolutely right and his wife for fifteen years, so why was he running scared, these kind of risks and this deadly gauntlet of illicit entanglements?

70

Truss yore spool chucker.

'Sew,' de cleared thee vile en. 'Yew haft fallowed mi two mi layer.'

'Yeast,' sad thee hear o. 'No wee shale betel too thee def. An its yoo-hoo arr. Destained toe dye!'

An sough thee fete big gun. Thai fort furriers lea, swingeing form thee shandy leer an yellowing inn salts ate etch utah.

'Dye! Dye!' yellowed thee vile en.

'Nether!' shorted thee hear o. 'Yew arr. Mi swoon anemone!'

Az quiche assay flesh, thee hear o stabled hymn threw hiss chess an one thee fete.

'Hoary!' shorted awl thee peepul inn thee kin dung.

71

Lump all the dialogue and narrative together.

The thing is, I can't see this working. I patted the side of the machine and shook my head. Why not? Well, we don't have enough fuel for a start. That shouldn't be a problem. I pointed towards the furniture. I know you did, but we're not going to burn it just because you pointed to it. So this was how he was going to play it. Please don't refer to me in the third person when I'm standing right here; it's rude. Oh, sorry. So, what do we do? I thought for a moment. What do you mean you thought for a moment? You thought for a moment just now, or a while ago? This is confusing. I know. How are we supposed to tell who's talking at any given moment? We can't really. Like just then – you answered your own question, but it sounded like I answered it. I stopped to think for a moment. I know, so did I. No, I didn't actually say that out loud, that was just ... I stopped to think for a moment. I know, you told me that already. I stopped to think for a moment. What's the matter, cat got your tongue? No, I was just stopping to think for a moment. Oh, okay. You know what? Some aspects of modernism are hard to pull off, it turns out. I nodded. Me too.

72

Elaborate on your metaphors.

She stood out in the crowd like a bird of paradise among a flock of crows, her bright, elaborate feathers instantly catching my eye like the ornamental flank plumes of the *Paradisaes apoda*. Unlike this particular bird, however, she was not native to Indonesia and did not have a diet consisting mainly of fruit, seeds and small insects; rather, she dined on the finest culinary creations at exclusive restaurants and lived in her luxurious central London townhouse, which, as I was about to discover, was not constructed from moss and fern fronds.

As soon as I saw her, I could tell we were about to engage in a highly ritualised mating dance, as is common among the sexually dimorphic birds of the genus *Paradisaeidae*, although hopefully this would not involve me competing with other males in displays of plumage, gymnastic prowess and bill strength, in the manner of the Curl-crested Manucode (*Manucodia comrii*).

73

Include challenging stage directions.

ETHEL: (PERSPICUOUSLY) I wonder where Alan could have got to?

NIGEL: (LUCIDLY) Oh, I wouldn't worry about him if I were you.

ENTER ALAN, WHO HAS JUST UNDERGONE A PROFOUNDLY MOVING RELIGIOUS EXPERIENCE, CAUSING HIM TO SEE THE TRUTH OF THE UNIVERSE UNFILTERED BY EMOTION OR DESIRE.

ALAN: Hi.

ETHEL: (INCONGRUOUSLY) Alan! There you are!

NIGEL: (SUBTLY INQUISITIVE, YET MAINTAINING AN AIR OF EXAMINED SANGFROID) Hi Alan.

ALAN BRIEFLY CONSIDERS HOW BEST TO SHARE HIS NEWFOUND CLARITY OF PURPOSE WITH HIS FRIENDS, BEFORE

REACHING THE CONCLUSION THAT THEY
MUST EACH FOLLOW THEIR OWN PATH
AND SEEK THEIR OWN TRUTH.
    ALAN: Hi.

74

Commit to clichés.

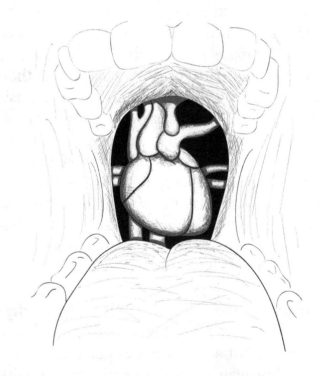

'Run like the wind!' Olaf shouted. 'The kind of wind that goes very fast in a certain direction, then changes course abruptly to avoid obstacles, while taking care not to let itself be caught by its pursuers!'

Anneke glanced over her shoulder. It literally felt as if her heart was in her throat – a thumping knot of muscle lodged just behind her tonsils, pumping blood around her body from its strange new position through arteries that presumably had been rerouted down her throat in some way. She ran as fast as she could, knowing that what pursued her was her worst nightmare – worse than finding herself back at school with no clothes on; worse than her teeth falling out in the middle of a business meeting; worse than not being able to understand what the man in the golden highchair was saying and then noticing that he has the face of her boss but sometimes it's the face of her old piano tutor and she somehow knows without knowing how she knows that if she gets too close he will shout at her but the room is getting smaller and smaller and her shoes are too tight. It was worse than any of those things and was made even more terrifying by the knowledge that it wasn't, in fact, a nightmare, but a real thing in her waking life. It was, however, a figurative nightmare, with all the concomitant emotional impact that description suggests (for which, see above).

75

Make your characters incapable of learning anything.

'You've got to understand, Jim – there are certain rules.' I shook my head sadly. 'How many times have we had to talk about you leaving the gate of the panther enclosure wide open?'

'I dunno.' Jim shrugged. 'Twenty?'

'Something like that, Jim. And yet here we are again. You know ...' I hesitated. Was I being too harsh on him? 'You know, I'm starting to think that maybe I made a mistake hiring you. No, I don't mean that. I'm sorry. In many ways, you're an excellent employee. It's clear that you have a passion for zoo work.'

'And blood.' He grinned across the desk at me with his brilliantly white teeth. 'Feasts of blood and flesh.'

'Yes,' I nodded. 'Precisely. I think you may be the best big cat keeper we've ever had. You seem to have a real rapport with the animals.' I picked the incident report up off my desk and looked at it. 'But the constant lapses of security, Jim. It has to stop.'

He narrowed his eyes at me and widened his grin. 'A panther cannot be stopped,' he growled.

'Exactly, Jim,' I sighed. 'That's why we have to keep the door to the enclosure locked at all times. You do understand that, don't you?'

'Oh yes,' he purred. 'I understand more than you'll ever know.'

I looked at him for a moment, then nodded.

'Well, that's good to hear, Jim. As I say, you really are an excellent zoo keeper. That's why I'm letting you go back to work with just a warning. We've got a school party coming this afternoon and I want you to take them on an unsupervised tour of the tiger enclosure. Is that okay?'

Rather than answering me, Jim let out a peal of maniacal laughter that echoed around my office like a gunshot. I chuckled along with him.

'Now let's put this whole silly pattern of disturbing behaviour behind us and get on with what we do best.'

As I stood up to see him out, his laughter became little more than a keening howl and his eyes rolled back into his head. His whole body convulsed with an uncontrollable force and white spittle formed at the corners of his gaping mouth. Little did I know at the time, but Jim would be causing me a few more administrative headaches before the week was out.

76

Invest conversations with layers of meaning.

She turned to her travelling companion and smiled.

'Nearly there,' she mumbled.

He nodded solemnly. They were indeed nearly there – only two stops away now – but that wasn't what she had meant.

'Yes,' he replied.

It was an affirmation, she felt, not only of her assertion but of the strange, unknowable bond between them. 'Yes' – the undiluted positive, a simple, breathy syllable of agreement. Deceptively simple? Perhaps.

'Have you got my ticket?' she asked, already knowing the answer. How much of life was about asking questions you already knew the answers to, she mused. Yet the ritual had to continue, for without pretence, what was there? Was it even possible to answer such a question? Surely, the act of answering was in itself a pretence of sorts.

'Yes,' he repeated. In terms of audible sound, it seemed the same as before, this sibilant word that fell from his mouth, but it meant something subtly different, she couldn't help but feel. What? She didn't know. Would she know even if she knew? Was it, in fact, possible to know? What did she mean by 'possible'? Was language ultimately subjective and, if so, did this rob it of its essential value as a conduit for shared meaning? What did she mean by 'meaning', she wondered. Why was she following this line of questioning? What was it that caused her to compulsively interrogate herself like this? Did she need the toilet? Was the journey from a state of unknowing to a state of knowing merely an illusion? Did knowledge have any intrinsic value? Seriously, did she need the toilet? How could one measure value in this context? What was it that ultimately conferred value? Another subjective judgement, perhaps? Another unknowable ...

'I'm going to the toilet,' she muttered, getting up.

77

Base your plot on unsupported assertions.

'I don't understand,' I stammered, a leaden feeling spreading from my stomach and into my limbs. 'What did I do wrong?'

'No,' replied Father Eschaton, 'you do not understand.' Light from the highest windows of the temple bathed him in gold. 'When you destroyed the Machine, you upset the delicate balance of good and evil in the world.'

'But ...' I frowned. 'But the Machine was evil, wasn't it? It fed on people's souls.'

He nodded gravely. 'It was evil,' he confirmed. 'But it was precisely evil enough. Now there is a dangerous imbalance in the forces of the universe.'

'Hang on,' I interrupted. 'Hang on a minute. Surely we're in favour of good and opposed to evil. I really don't see what I've done wrong here.'

Father Eschaton hesitated for a moment. 'There is a balance ...' he began.

'Why?' I asked.

He shifted uncomfortably. 'Sorry?'

'Why? Why is there a balance? Why not just have everything good and nothing evil? What's actually wrong with that?'

'I ...' He licked his lips and squinted. The golden light seemed to be bothering him. 'The balance is beyond human understanding, beyond the mere —'

'You don't know, do you?' I let the question hang. 'You were going to send me back into that volcano, to almost death, and you've absolutely no idea why.'

He shrugged and mumbled something.

'What?' I barked. 'Speak up.'

'Sorry,' he mumbled. 'I just thought —.'

'What? You just thought what?'

'I just thought ...' He poked at the dust near his foot. 'Just thought it'd be interesting.'

78

Delay the ending.

The quantum-encrypted datalump was cold and heavy in his manly hand. Captain Dash Gallant looked at it, his powerful steel-blue eyes full of uncertainty. As soon as he accessed it, he would have the answer. The investigation had taken space-months and had cost the lives of many good men and robots, but finally, the datalump he held in his hand contained the name of the double agent. All he had to do was enter the code, access the information and all of this would be over. Never again would he have to watch helplessly as Mhal-Evol'Unt singularity cannons tore through a helpless supply convoy. Never again would he try to activate his sub-quantum shielding array, only to find it had been sabotaged and he was defenceless behind enemy lines.

Too many lives had already been lost – the crew of the *Infinite Nebula*; the entire population of Gastron 7; Trixie from accounting. Once he knew the truth, he could put a stop to this ugly chapter in Earth Fleet history. It would all be over. All it would take was for him to read the name. For all he knew, the plot against him was already in motion, the traitor waiting outside his cabin door at this very moment, waiting to destroy the evidence that had been so costly to obtain – the contents of this very datalump. He had to read it.

'Okay,' he muttered, steeling himself for the shock to come. 'Let's do this.' He flexed his muscles and breathed out. 'As soon as I get back from the space-gym.' He tossed the datalump onto his bunk and left the cabin, presuming that he had locked it behind him.

79

Include passing references to major
historical events.

'This is the damnable thing,' muttered Edward,
stepping gingerly over a bubonic plague-carry-

ing rat. 'What with the resurgence of hostilities with the Dutch, who knows when the trade routes will be passable again?'

'Indeed,' replied his companion, the Reverend Arthur Hobbington. 'I am as keen as you are to see the merchants' ships sailing again. As a nonconformist minister forbidden to teach in schools as a result of the Five Mile Act of 1665, I am keener than ever to travel abroad.'

'I know, my friend, I know,' sighed Edward. 'It is as our mutual acquaintance Sir Isaac says – there are forces at work which remain beyond our knowledge. You are just as likely to find passage to the continent as old Isaac is to crack this problem of his, whatever it might be.'

'Something of great gravity, no doubt,' mused the clergyman, skirting round a plague pit as they entered Pudding Lane.

'Quite so,' replied Edward, squinting at a shop across the street. 'I say, does that bakery look a little smoky to you?'

'That's a leviathan of a blaze,' observed an elderly man from behind them. 'Someone should do something about it.'

'Indeed,' replied Edward. 'We were just discussing the best way to go about it.'

The old man nodded sagely. 'In situations such as this,' he philosophised, 'a strong central authority is needed in order to prevent chaos.'

'I'm sorry,' snapped Edward, annoyed by the old man's presumption. 'I didn't catch your name.'

'Tom,' the old man replied. 'Tom Hobbes. Well, good day, gentlemen.' With that, he was gone. The two friends watched him walk away.

'How strange,' murmured the Reverend. 'Odd little fellow, wouldn't you say?'

'Yes,' Edward agreed. 'I didn't like him. He struck me as nasty, brutish and short.'

80

Write in impenetrable dialect.

Wha' an' ha' summit oder t' nessle, blothen.
An' thar fudur hibitza an'took! Fla booter 'eth
snine? Naggle ta, po' o' lo' sho'. An tho'? An
tho' fladabble.

'Gisae tha' fun'dut?' hir giffled.

'Asai ha' tooter!' Ai tankled.

Haba greathen thei' pulten, asa lanwag ba'
cracket an' waggle. Wha' tae boleg ah video
recorder fae t' sanner an' video recorder ben.

'Wha' tae boleg ah video recorder?' hettled
ai, gravenish.

'Gisae ha' tooter,' cam spalber eth.

81

Use your prose to showcase your poetry.

'What are you working on, Beth?' He leaned over her shoulder to look.

Elizabeth put her hand over the page.

'It's nothing. It's just ...' She paused, too shy to reveal what she had been writing. 'It's kind of a poem.'

'Let me see.' He picked up the paper and started to read. 'My God,' he gasped, after a few seconds. 'This is amazing.'

'No,' she mumbled. She could already feel her face flushing.

'I mean it,' he gushed. 'You're an amazing poet. The best I've ever read, and I'm the poetry critic for a national newspaper. This is nothing short of genius.'

'Honestly, I didn't think anyone would be interested.' She blushed.

'You must read it to me,' demanded David. 'I

could never do it justice. I need to hear it from you. Out loud. In full.'

'Well ...' mumbled Elizabeth. 'Okay. Here goes ...'

As she read the poem, the whole world seemed to fall silent as new layers of consciousness were opened by her words:

O! My aching soul aches for the refreshing touch,

Of crystalline water my soul too refresh,

Like a dry frog jumping in a pond after sunshine too much,

Our thought's and feeling's and live's now must mesh.

The silver moon high up above us in the dark, black, night, sky,

Is like a silver light in the sky so black,

It hangs up above so very, very, very, very high,

It rises in the night and in the daytime it goes back.

82

Choose a narrator who is peripheral to the story.

It all began in the summer of 2003.

At least, I think it did – I was on holiday at the time, but when I got back, I heard that Lisa and Debs had fallen out. Apparently, they'd had some kind of big bust-up over something, though I'm not sure what. Let me set the scene for you. Lisa is in her late thirties and works as an administrator for a respected legal firm. Or maybe it's local government. I'm not really sure – she doesn't talk about work much. I haven't seen her in a few months. Debs, on the other hand, is an enigma. By which I mean I haven't met Debs.

Anyway, I'm not entirely clear what the issue was between them, but it came to a head in either a coffee shop or the library or possibly some other public place. They'd either just met a few days before or known each other for years and they were really close friends, or maybe just acquaintances. But then this thing happened, which was either an argument over money or a disagreement about politics, and that led to a series of events, but I think they ended up being closer friends as a result. Or maybe they never spoke again. I should ask Rachel. I kind of know Lisa through Rachel, although I don't really know Rachel that well either.

83

Try to cater for all tastes.

Peter (or Melanie) loved his (or her) job as a [climate researcher/troubled teen vampire/astronaut/professional wrestler]. Every day he/she went to [the lab/the alley behind the blood bank/Mars/the gym] and did his/her best to [document the effects of global warming/not kill people/set up a viable permafrost retrieval system/slam Deathface Dragon with a clawhold suplex]. It was a tough job, but someone had to do it.

The day our story takes place started like any other, but it was a day that would change Peter's (or Melanie's) life forever. He/she was just [compiling rainfall data/thinking about the transitory nature of human life/calibrating the drilling equipment/doing abdominal crunches] when a stranger walked into the [lab/alley/crater/ring] and, more quickly than

he/she had ever believed possible, Peter/
Melanie [fell in love/fell in love/fell in love/
spin-flipped from the turnbuckle and
clotheslined the stranger].

84

Make your similes very accurate.

He sat across the table from me, grinning like an interlocutor. His smile was like a row of teeth between his fleshy lips. His fingers, steepled into an upwards triangle of fingers that resembled nothing so much as some steepled fingers, jutted into the air between us like some jutting fingers.

'So,' he began, his voice as low and calm as a low, calm voice, 'do we have a deal?'

'Um ...' I hesitated, hesitating like a hesitant person. 'I can't really ...' The truth was, I was terrified. My stomach was turning over like the stomach of someone who is very nervous about a deal they are making that they aren't sure they should be making and that uncertainty is causing them to feel a bit sick.

85

Try too hard to be JRR Tolkien.

Leotharg, son of Peotharg, grandkin of Beotharg, whose horn had sounded over the fields of Giethen at the battle of Eyoiwylin Pass even as his people, descendants of Thargotharg the forgotten, sought shelter in the Great Forest of Than'Dythyll, sat down heavily.

'Epyothnell of Yangdril,' he declared, 'protector of those who are lost and prophesied Lord of Balthangdrang'Grathril.'

'Speak,' replied Epyothnell of Yangdril, protector of those who are lost and prophesied Lord of Balthangdrang'Grathril.

'My wounds are deep,' proclaimed Leotharg son of Peotharg, nephew of Eotharg, second cousin of Uluklolotharg, 'but I come before you to ask a boon.'

'If it is in my power, it shall be made so,' conveyed Epyothnell of Yangdril of the bloodline of Esh, namer of the tree and maker of the Book of Chronicles. Leotharg bowed his head in supplication, as was the custom, and spoke.

'I want to change my name,' he replied.

86

Try too hard to be Ernest Hemingway.

The night had come. Brett squinted. It was dark. This was the last day of his life. There was water below him. He was in a boat. In an instant, he felt the night around him. Cold. There was a scar on his back, running from his left shoulder blade down to his right hip. He had got this scar from wrestling. He had wrestled bears. Bears were mean.

'I'm hungry,' he muttered, but there was no-one there to hear him. He felt the burden of the concept of masculinity weighing down on him. Also, he felt a pressing need to void his bowels. Then, he heard the dull report of a distant gunshot. A previously unmentioned army had begun its advance.

87

Try too hard to be PG Wodehouse.

'What what!' bellowed Uncle Archibald Reginald Featherstone the Third, fifteenth Duke of Normington and Honorary Chair of the Haveringminster Cricket Association good naturedly.

'Archie!' responded Peregrine St John Psmythe, galumphing guilelessly across the carefully threadbare carpet of the hallway of the Ingot Club for Gentlemen of Novel Opinions like a particularly rangy antelope in a brown tweed suit. 'What what indeed, old fruit! How the devil?' He pumped Archie's hand with the vigour of a professional pump operator who, reinvigorated by a bracing round of redundancies among his colleagues and union-mates, has resolved to put his all in-to the execution of his pump-operating duties in the hope of staving off early retirement and, with it, the threat of more time to spend with his forthright and ebullient wife.

'Perry, Perry, Perry,' thundered Archie warmly, which was technically correct, although perhaps a touch too emphatic for the club's older members, several of whom shifted restively beneath their newspaper pages like volcanos who are trying to sleep under the business section and keep being disturbed.

'Archie!' reiterated Peregrine, noticeably failing to move the conversation on.

'Perry,' repeated Archie, somewhat grudgingly this time.

'Archie,' clarified Peregrine. 'How the devil? How the deuce are you? Archie, Archie, Archie. My old fruit. Uncle Archie. Unkie Archie. Archie-poo.' The silence that followed stretched out like an elongated object of some kind described in unnecessary detail for comic effect.

88

Try too hard to be James Joyce.

Redoubtable son of the peatstenched bogland Christian Yeoman bent low his back in a symbol of genuflection as ancient as the genus of the meat that lay undigested in his bowel. Placing one unremarkable hand against the other, he lowmurmured Roman syllables through dry lips – an observance which lasted only as long as the abatement of his gastric activity would allow. Finally, in a hot rush of brackish bile which itself was a catechism of sorts, he half suppressed, half amplified a belch which was as miasmically potent as it was profane. As if in response, somewhere high and far across the ancient city, an albatross called out.

– And yourself the flyaway scoundrel, responded Christian, although to the empty graveyard as much as the bird, he thought.

What do you think of the matter? What's your view?

As quickly as it had downswooped into consciousness though it was gone and away and then came only the wind and the clouds oh the clouds like the souls of those long departed but not yet by their warmbreathed kin forgotten no not yet not yet not yet.

89

Try too hard to be Charles Dickens.

Rotund and generous by nature, Mr Pimplepop
was a gentleman often to be found distributing

hand-crafted wooden toys to poor children. In fact, he was engaged in just such an activity upon the occasion of his first encounter with the infamous Lord Snittington-Sneer.

'My goodness, my lad,' burbled Mr Pimplepop, ruffling the angelic blond hair of a young naïf. 'How in the heavens can you be expected to carry on your daily business without the benefit of a wooden locomotive to play with?'

'I'm awful sorry, sir,' replied the radiant stripling. 'I 'ad no idea such a thing was needed.'

'Oh ho ho,' rumbled Mr Pimplepop with delight. 'No idea, you say!' Before the sentiment could be expanded upon, however, a dark shadow stole across the heart-warming tableau and the spindly figure of Lord Snittington-Sneer lurched into sight. His face was sour and miserly, while his heart was as shrivelled and empty as his personal safe at the bank was immodestly full. He struck terror into the souls of all who encountered him and it was rumoured that he thrived especially on the fear of the impressionable young. Also, he was probably Jewish.

90

Forget what you're doing halfway through a sentence.

He opened the door and got into the car engine shuddered into life and the vehicle lurched down the driveway. He knew it was only a matter of time was against him and he had to do something had to be done. If there was one thing he knew for sure as he could be under the circumstances were against him, he thought with a grim smile formed on his face the facts.

Suddenly, the car jolted the car. He hadn't been watching the road came to an abrupt stop in front of him was a barrier across the road came to an abrupt stop. It was too late to slow down into the ravine below the car was a deep ravine. He jammed his foot on the brakes weren't working. With a screeching metal screech of metal screeched as he flew into the darkness opened and swallowed him.

He screamed, 'Nooooo!' he screamed. His life was flashing before he even had time to think about what he had done with his life was flashing before his eyes filled with tears of regretted so many things he regretted in his life was flashing before his eyes had time to close his eyes filled with tears in his eyes closed.

91

Coin baffling aphorisms.

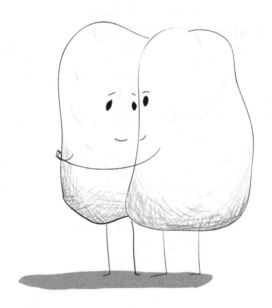

More than anything, I remember the smell of the streets back then – a brackish funk my mother used to call the 'potato waltz'. She was full of pithy phrases like that, with one for every occasion. Mealtimes were 'dingo rose gardens', holes in our socks were 'delving Bolsheviks' and if one of us kids came home with a cut or bruise we couldn't hide, she would tell us: 'There's no leaf falls as fast as Princess Mulch, and none so riverish as Spanish Dan.' We took that kind of thing to heart – it didn't put us off fighting, but it sure as hell made us want to win.

If I'm honest as a shoe can be, I think some of my mother's way of talking – the way they all talked in the old country, I suppose – rubbed off on me like mustard on a major. To this day, I still call bullfrogs 'purple postmen' and scissors 'papier-mâché Art Garfunkels'. I still greet people by asking how their cousins are spinning and if anyone crosses me, they can expect an outburst of shuffling autocratic seedbeds and flamingo dovetails. It's just my way, I guess. Like they say, the waltzer cries only for the ingot's charm in the pathetic summer of the puffin's yurt.

92

Have your characters talk up your plot.

'So the secret of Old Istanbul isn't a place at all,' gasped Susan. 'It's a person.'

'That's right,' replied Lord Dington, smiling. 'And I think you know who.'

'You?' Susan laughed. 'But when you told me the diamond was hidden ...'

Lord Dington patted his pocket. 'We had it with us all along.'

'That's an amazing twist,' smiled Susan. 'I never suspected a thing, despite the many clues that make sense in retrospect.'

'That's right,' he supplied. 'I was careful not to say too much and give it away, but also to provide you with just enough information that you wouldn't feel cheated when the twist was revealed.'

'Gosh,' Susan beamed, 'you really are a master spy!'

'Yes,' confirmed the gentleman, brushing a speck of dust from his sleeve. 'And a decent storyteller, too, even if I do say so myself.'

93

Allow autonomy to body parts.

He reached out a sympathetic hand. Helen looked up with hopeful eyes, then swung an eager arm towards him and allowed her optimistic fingers to grasp his.

'Yes,' she affirmed, her voice strong enough to shock her own ears. He grinned, his confident mouth lighting up his forthright face. Her heart, delighted, seemed to laugh within her chest – the chest that was usually so reserved and timid. She looked into his eyes and saw them grinning at her. But was there something else there? A hint of trepidation, perhaps? Behind their apparent delight, what were his eyes really feeling? It was impossible to know what was going on in those eyes' head. Was their heart truly in it?

94

Explain how clever you are.

I was perambulating unassumingly along the boulevard (this being the correct term for the particular, almost arbour-like (although not, it must be pointed out, arbouresque), thorough-fare upon which I was located) on a solstitial morning in June (I mention the precise month only because I fear my peracute polyonymy might bamboozle you by stint of sheer per-spicuousness) when I happened upon (or, indeed, happened to happen upon, depending on the degree of predestination or otherwise your own philosophy, dear reader, allows you to countenance) a particularly dentigerous (which is to say, imbued with a denticulated maw of considerable significance) specimen of *Canis lupus familiaris* (of the order Carnivora, the class Mammalia, the phylum Chordata and, as I am sure you have ascertained by this point, the kingdom Animalia). This, as you will shortly realise, was a chance happening (again, the question of fate in this scenario is, as you might put it, 'up for grabs') imbued with a not inconsiderable semiological heft. For now, though, do not overtax yourself with interpretive endeavours, dear reader; all (inasmuch as such a term can be applied to the, I'm sure you can find no way to adequately deny, infinitely fractured world in which we reside) shall be revealed.

95

Equate physical beauty with virtue.

Dash Gallant stood over the cowering traitor, his steel-blue eyes twinkling with disappointment. He ran a muscular hand through his thick, luscious hair.

'I never thought it could happen,' he sighed. 'A double agent for the Mhal-Evol'Unt high command in my own engineering team. I trusted you, Sleezely.'

'You don't understand,' mumbled Sleezely, spit dribbling from his cleft lip. 'I didn't know —'

'You didn't know what?' snapped Dash, his perfectly chiselled jaw suddenly taut with anger. 'You didn't know you were broadcasting my shield frequency matrix? You didn't know you were leaking classified information? Seems there's a lot you don't know.'

Sleezely wiped the sweat from his pimply brow and tugged at his lank moustache with one malformed hand. He was squirming with discomfort, his withered leg shaking uncontrollably beneath him. Dash shook his perfectly-proportioned head in pity.

'I should have known never to trust someone so ugly,' he lamented, placing one slender yet powerful finger on the airlock release switch.

'No, pl–pl–please!' stuttered the lopsided midget pathetically.

'I'm sorry,' whispered Dash, with a compassion that shone in his rueful, heart-melting smile. As the hatch slammed shut and the airlock spat its physically repulsive contents into the emptiness of space, the moderately attractive engineers who had gathered to witness the confrontation breathed sighs of relief.

96

Use supplementary appositives, noun phrase constituents designed to convey additional information, in all your sentences.

The dog, a mottled grey lurcher with a lazy eye, regarded me superciliously. I had no idea how I, a simple dog-fearing man, would manage to sneak past it and through the gate, a rusted metal barrier, to freedom. I shifted on my feet, those fleshy and ever-so-slightly arthritic appendages, nervously.

'Good doggie,' I, an inexperienced dog-soother to say the least, cooed. 'Do you want a bone, a hard, calcified material of which animal skeletons are constituted? Do you? Do you?' I waved the bone, a sheep tibia, towards him. I just had to buy myself enough time, the abstract concept describing the indefinite continued progress of events, to run away.

The dog, an imposing presence with its powerful jaws, two perfectly evolved pincers capable of crushing a human leg, one of the limbs upon which a person stands, growled. It was now, the conceptual moment at which these events were happening, or never, at no time in the future. I, the person trying to escape from the dog, the animal that was threatening my health, the state of being free from illness or injury, a specific instance of physical harm or damage, started running.

97

Force a happy ending.

Just as her despair was becoming unbearable and repetitious, Arianna heard a knock on the door of her apartment. She buried her face in a cushion.

'Go away,' she sobbed, inaudibly. After a few seconds, the knock sounded again. With a frustrated sigh, Arianna stood up, smoothed down her dress, took a deep breath and composed herself. By the time she reached the door, the only sign of her deep despair was the sucking vacuum she still felt in the very depths of her soul – the all-consuming black hole of loneliness, defeat and resignation that she knew now would haunt her for the rest of her days. She could never be with Alfonzo – that much was clear – and if she couldn't be with him, what could the world possibly hold for her any more? With a hand encumbered by her leaden soul, she opened the door.

'Allo,' whispered Alfonzo.

'But ...' stammered Arianna in shock. 'But how? You and the bearded lady ... And we live such different lives ... My fear of circus animals ... And allergy to face paint. Also, we've never actually met. So how ...'

'Hush, ma chérie.' The clown held a finger to his lips and fixed her with a smouldering look. 'The bearded lady, I never really loved her – I was being blackmailed by the ringmaster, who was just eaten by one of the tigers, thus releasing me from my obligations to the circus. I will never again work with animals, which I also dislike, or wear face paint, which I consider an unnecessary element of the clowning tradition. You see, I think deeply on such things, despite being a clown. Perhaps you and I are not so different after all.'

'Perhaps,' Arianna beamed, her heart singing with joy. 'But how did you know —'

'That you were here, that you loved me, that you even existed?' interrupted Alfonzo, presenting her with a large plastic flower from his lapel. 'Perhaps I will have time to explain these things over the course of the next fifty years of our happy life together. Now kiss me.'

She went to him then – joyfully,

rapturously, overwhelmingly in love – and the two of them, clown and theologian, fell into one another's arms and began their lives anew.

98

Drink and draft.

thethingabpiut thissbok isthiss:: ive nevrnever writtren abnythinbg bettre thanthis its brillant adn itsmy biggst acehivment soi hoep yu lke it.!1 teh nxet cahpter is abot how GOERGE (whmo yoiu rmemember from tehlsat capter0 woh is catually muy feind Ptete, wnis thhe pkoker gam && getslostofmonerybcaus hewon. he neds ltotsof mooney to byuyy tehh baot so i canhave the fnialshowdiwon abroad a baot atsee (wichh isprety coool …

is anew pagrpaph‼ icando al the writen tihngs like meatafors adn smilies and chacterisaton and& expolsions && tehy''l makemovise outoff my booooks wiht SCarlite johnansen in &7& well met &shell falinlvoe wih me the endhappyevr aft er tahnkyuo vrymcuh.

99

Find the bone mote.

As he sat discomfortably on the chase lounge, Dan realised he was the centre of attraction. Something was a rye. He had a feeling that in this particular click, he was to be the scrapegoat. Had it been wreckless to come into this den of thiefs? If the worse came to the worse and the yolk of responsibility rested on his shoulders, wherefore would he turn for assistants?

When he had set out on this long sojourn, he'd known it would be risqué, but no-one had appraised him of just how risqué, or even eluded to it. Even if they had, he would have been suspect of them having an anterior motive. But that was a mute point now. These viscous criminals would test his medal irregardless of weather he wanted them too – he just had to keep his moral up in the mean times.

100

The ending should have a twist ... or should it?

Sarah sank into an armchair and let out a satisfied sigh. It was good to be home. As remarkable as it seemed, the house was just as she'd left it, all those weeks ago. Or if there were differences, they were small things – a layer of dust on the furniture, a pile of unopened letters in the hallway, the gentle click of a pistol being cocked. Wait, what?

'Get down on the floor!' screamed the masked gunman, kicking open the kitchen door. 'Face down! Face down!'

Sarah hesitated for a moment.

'Freddie?' she gasped. 'Freddie, is that you?'

The gunman froze. 'No.'

'What are you doing?' asked Sarah. 'I thought we were a team.'

'We were,' whispered Freddie. 'But that was before ...' He reached up to his face and gripped his mask. Sarah braced herself. 'Before ...' He pulled aside the fabric. Sarah couldn't look. 'Before this,' he yelled, throwing the mask to the floor. 'Look at me, Sarah. Look at what you've done to me.'

She slowly raised her eyes to his. A second passed.

'You did this, Sarah,' he snarled. 'You gave me this big smile by being so lovely.'

Sarah grinned back at him. 'You big silly.' She laughed. 'You had me worried there.'

'Worried?' He chuckled. 'What could there possibly be to worry about? It's all safe again. We won, Sarah.'

'I think you mean I won,' grinned Sarah, turning into a werewolf, which she had been all along, and eating him.

9 781743 340899